ENDING DOMESTIC VIOLENCE CAPTIVITY

A GUIDE TO ECONOMIC FREEDOM

DR. LUDY GREEN

volcanopress.com

Ending Domestic Violence Captivity: A Guide to Economic Freedom

Copyright © 2014 by Ludy Green, Ph.D.

All Rights Reserved. No part of this book may be copied or reproduced by any means, electronic or mechanical, including photocopying, recording, or any information storage and retrieval system, without prior permission in writing by the publisher.

Library of Congress Cataloging-in-Publication Data

Green, Ludy.

Ending domestic violence captivity : a guide to economic freedom / Ludy Green, Ph.D.

　　pages　　cm

Includes bibliographical references.

ISBN-13: 978-1-884244-41-4 (hc)

ISBN-13: 978-1-884244-38-4 (pbk.)

ISBN-10: 1-884244-38-6 (eb)

1. Family violence. 2. Victims of family violence—Services for. 3. Sexual abuse victims—Services for. 4. Abused women—Employment. I. Title.

HV6626.G743 2014

362.82'9282—dc23　　　　　　　　　　　　　　　　　　　　　　2014004307

Cover design: Jeff Brandenburg
Interior page design: Jeff Brandenburg
Editor: Leigh Ann Ross

Published by Volcano Press
Box 270
Volcano, CA 95689
For ordering: www.volcanopress.com

First Volcano Press printing, 2014

Printed in the United States of America

For my beloved Aunt Melba, who was a constant source of encouragement and love.

Contents

From the Publisher vii

Acknowledgments ix

Note xi

Prologue xiii

Introduction xvii

PART ONE
The Core Problem: Domestic Disempowerment 1

CHAPTER 1	From Inner Void to Inner Voice 3
CHAPTER 2	The Direction of Dreams 17
CHAPTER 3	Why She Stays . . . and Why We Ask 29
CHAPTER 4	Contrary Theories 39
CHAPTER 5	Domestic Captivity 45
CHAPTER 6	Domestic Tyranny 53
CHAPTER 7	True Stories of Domestic Captivity 57
CHAPTER 8	Forms of Abuse 81
CHAPTER 9	Forms of Abuse Continued: Economic Abuse 85
CHAPTER 10	Domestic Disempowerment 97
CHAPTER 11	Processes of Disempowerment 105
CHAPTER 12	Human Trafficking 115

PART TWO
A Solution That Lasts: Power in the Pursuit of Dreams 121

CHAPTER 13	The Meaning of Empowerment 123
CHAPTER 14	The Purpose of Employment and the Employment of Purpose . . 127
CHAPTER 15	In Practice: Operations of Second Chance 133
CHAPTER 16	Mounting Up on Wings: True Stories of Lasting Freedom 161
CHAPTER 17	The New VAWA and the Second Chance Provision 177

Endnotes 181

About the Author 185

From the Publisher

There is a certain synchronicity to publishing . . . 'bookends' in the literary world, if you want a visual aid. I published the first book on domestic violence in the United States in 1976, *Battered Wives* by Del Martin. As groundbreaking a book as that was nearly 40 years ago, sadly—the message then still applies today. The issue of family violence hasn't diminished . . . but thankfully, the legion of dedicated people with empirical knowledge addressing this problem has increased.

Perhaps it is best to admit that the universal problem of domestic violence may *never* be solved. But assuming that is the case, it then becomes a question of where one must apply their own unique set of skills to try and abate this horrific phenomenon. As poet Gary Snyder once said, "*Find your place on the planet, dig in and take responsibility from there.*"

Therefore, I am proud of the many books Volcano Press has published to give a voice to the victim and then, I hope...the survivor... and ultimately the woman who thrives in a purposeful life, elevated beyond the hands of her abuser. Many of our books have been utilized by professionals in the field of domestic violence—and even better yet, many of our books have been adapted for curriculum at the university level for courses on sociology, health care, criminology and women's studies. We applaud the many outstanding professionals who have devoted their work to end the scourge that is violence against women.

Thus, it is with great pride that Volcano Press publishes *Ending Domestic Violence Captivity: A Guide to Economic Freedom*, the story of Dr. Ludy Green and the organization she founded, *Second Chance Employment Services* (SCES) based in Washington, DC.

Dr. Green saw the correlation between helping abused women gain financial independence, and thus moving closer to freedom from their abusers. We all know that the reasons women choose to stay with the man who inflicts violence upon them are complex—but financial dependence is one of the largest factors.

To assist women entering the work place for the first time, or to getting them *to return* to the work force—is a milestone step. The battered women's movement has collectively talked long and hard about the issues related to abuse and why it happens. Herein is a model for a solution. An argument can be made that if *one woman* escapes a violent relationship because she was able to go through SCES, secure a job, and thereby escaping the confines of her abuser . . . the work of Ludy Green could be considered significant. That she has helped hundreds of women is remarkable.

From providing presentable clothing and accessories, plastic surgery where her physical appearance has been scarred by an abuser, to addressing the poise and confidence required for a good interview, SCES is filling a great void for women in transition.

Ludy Green's partnership with many corporate entities in the U.S. is a testament to the success rate of her program, and an inspiration to others. She has been recognized by Congress for her remarkable achievements and she is showing no signs of slowing down.

In publishing Ludy Green's book, Volcano Press is fulfilling a dream that began in 1976—of bringing vital information and awareness about domestic violence to the world. We are proud of our contribution.

We also thank Women and Children's Support Resources (wcsr.org) for their invaluable partnership with Volcano Press in producing the first printing of this book, made possible through a private donation.

—**Ruth Gottstein**, *Publisher, Volcano Press*

Acknowledgments

There are no words to adequately express the depth of my gratitude to my loving husband Joe and my dearest daughter Megan. Without their patience, support and limitless love through many hours, days and years, this work could never have been accomplished.

A heartfelt thanks goes out to Senator Bob Dole, my lifelong mentor, for his genuine commitment in joining me in the fight against domestic violence.

Special thanks to Manpower's [former president] David Arkless for believing in my vision and for his support in partnering with Second Chance to expand the organization nationally and internationally.

I am especially grateful for my business mentors, Georgette Mosbacher (member of Second Chance's Board of Directors) and Arianna Huffington (serves on Second Chance's Board of Advisors).

I am also grateful to all the members of the Second Chance Board of Directors. In addition to those already mentioned they are: Ron Perlman, M.D.; Constance Battle, M.D.; the Honorable H. Mark Kennedy; Rich Massabny; Commissioner Carol A. Roberts; Kevin A. Ryan, D.D.S.; Commissioner Barbara Sheen-Todd; and my dearest professor, Joseph Zeidner, Ph.D.

I extend my special thanks to Roger Banks, Esq. for his research and editing.

Thank you to Gina Varolli for her assistance with the surveys of Second Chance clients.

Katy Duboeuf and Benjamin Duboeuf of Cristophe Salon in Washington, DC, have my gratitude and my admiration for their over-the-top generosity in donating superb talent every week to serve Second Chance clients. Their faithfulness in this commitment is awe-inspiring.

Special thanks to my faithful friend, Miriam Galloway.

Thank you to my dear friend and partner in the fight against domestic violence, Kim Wells, Executive Director of the Corporate Alliance to End Partner Violence.

Thank you to my sister Pam "Pammy" Rembaum for always being here for me—no matter what.

No expression of gratitude would be complete without inclusion of my remarkable publisher Ruth Gottstein, founder of Volcano Press, and a pioneer in publishing books on domestic violence and other issues facing women and children. For believing in me, and for allowing me this space to tell the good news of lifelong freedom from domestic violence, I could never thank her enough.

Finally, I am grateful for the many partners, donors and volunteers, whose donations of time, talent and treasure have helped Second Chance Employment Services become a solution to domestic violence victims.

Note

Biographical Details Changed to Protect Identities.

The biographical narratives of a number of the author's former clients are included in these pages for illustrative purposes. To protect the safety and privacy of individuals involved, certain identifying facts (names, dates, locations, etc.) have been modified.

Prologue

In the documentary "America's Heart and Soul," a film sequence begins with a close-up shot of a bald eagle. Its iconic pearl head is thrust forward; its wings gleam with vitality and power. The bird is held in talon-proof gloves by an elder of the Alaskan Tlingit Indian Tribe. The Tlingit have a history of success in rescuing wounded eagles. They shelter the animals and treat their injuries until they're strong enough to return to the wild.

The man's arms swing upward, his gloves disappear in a feathery blur, and the eagle is gone. The camera cuts to show the bird ascending past a row of telephone poles, over evergreens, and upwards still. Finally, above an expansive Alaskan landscape, the eagle soars majestically in the sun-drenched sky. The climax is accompanied by the elder's voice-over narration:

> When we rescue an injured eagle, and nurture her back to health, she will fly once again, and gets a second chance. . . . It's like watching a great spirit of freedom. . . .

The eagle "gets a second chance," meaning its injuries have not sealed it's fate. For me, the term "second chance" has a special significance because it echoes the name I chose for my charitable organization, Second Chance Employment Services, founded many years before this film was made. The mission of Second Chance is to restore the spirit of women who have been profoundly injured by domestic violence. The shared term evokes certain symbolic connections between the eagle's release and the work of Second Chance.

Domestic violence victims come to Second Chance severely injured, physically and psychologically. Having been subjected to terrible oppression and brutality, they want nothing more than to be free. Yet voices around them, and often their own inner voice, have convinced them there is no hope of escape, no way to improve their circumstances. Second Chance's long track record of success proves they can indeed escape the violence and oppression and begin a new life free from abuse.

In the documentary, the purpose of the eagle's rescue is not only to treat its injuries. Another purpose is to return the eagle to its natural place, to set it free. Second Chance was founded with an analogous goal. Beyond helping them to survive and recover from physical and psychological wounds, the organization exists to enable survivors to live in total freedom from violent relationships, even as they pursue their own independent aspirations and dreams.

Another parallel lies in the way the eagle returns to the wild. To leave the rescuer's hands, to climb higher and finally to soar, the eagle uses the natural strength of its own wings. Initially, the creature had to depend on its rescuers. Without their expert diagnosis, treatment, and care, it could not have recovered. But when strength to live independently is restored, it flies to freedom on its own power.

The system pioneered by Second Chance is fundamentally a system of empowerment. It often happens that a woman is referred to us after she's been mistreated with unimaginable cruelty at the hands of a domestic partner. Her challenges may seem insurmountable. Following a step-by-step process, she is helped by, then enabled to let go of, graduated forms of support, tailored to her specific needs. Ultimately, Second Chance does not carry her to freedom. Second Chance *releases* her to freedom. The survivor is empowered to fly, as it were, on the power of her own wings.

Finally, the Tlingit's phrase, "great spirit of freedom" rings true as a metaphor because the eagle's release from the shelter is permanent. Never turning back, the very emblem of independence resumes its rightful place in the sky. If the release were temporary, if the flight ended with a descending spiral back to the shelter, the beauty of the scene, with its triumphal music and magnificent footage, would be lost. In fact, there would be no scene.

The primary goal of Second Chance is the same: freedom that lasts. Our emphasis on permanence is one of the things that sets Second Chance's method apart. Although temporary services for protection and healing are absolutely essential, they are not, in the end, sufficient. Second Chance is aimed at the underlying problems of domestic captivity and tyranny. The services are specifically designed to help her avoid being drawn back into the injurious relationship. So, when a survivor is released by Second Chance, I imagine the fulfillment of an ancient scripture: they "shall renew their strength; they shall mount up with wings as eagles."[1]

Introduction

Until recently, scientific studies of economic abuse in domestic violence have been few and far between. Among the first to notice the paucity of such research was Professor Adrianne E. Adams, in her 2008 article published in the journal *Violence Against Women*:

> Although a great deal of research to date has examined the prevalence and consequences of physical, psychological and sexual abuse, economic abuse has received far less attention from the scientific community. . . .[2]

Adams goes on to explain the purpose of her study:

> to . . . enable researchers to examine the nature and extent of this form of abuse; the impact that it has on women's economic, physical and mental health; and the implications that it has on the women's ability to escape abusive partners. With a richer understanding of economic abuse, we can begin to develop interventions and tailor existing programming to the unique experiences and needs of women whose financial health has been compromised by an abusive partner.[3]

The study is a welcome scholarly affirmation of the approach Second Chance had begun implementing in 2001, through a program to counteract economic abuse and its harmful effects.

Second Chance was the first (and remains today the only) employment agency designed specifically for victims of domestic violence and other types of exploitation and abuse. The system developed by Second Chance for the economic empowerment of survivors of domestic abuse has established a track record of success. It has so far led nearly 900 women to lifelong freedom from abusive partners. The system has proven uniquely effective in breaking what has been regarded as a difficult to break "cycle of violence." It is now also being used to liberate victims of the modern-day slavery epidemic that is human trafficking.

The inspiration and innovation of Second Chance grew out of my experiences as a volunteer at a battered woman's shelter. There I became passionate about finding a solution to the problem I encountered: victims of violence leaving the shelter after a period of safety only to return to the abusive household. Second Chance began as an experiment to address what I view as the core problem of domestic violence: the victim's' inability to terminate the relationship. We aren't talking about a run-of-the mill "feeling trapped" experience, as may occur in even healthy relationships. Here it's a different kind of captivity. In my mind, it is a veritable prison. The bars are invisible and all but unbreakable. They are made of the cumulative impact of physical, verbal, economic and other abuses.

In the years since Second Chance's founding, the experiment has proven successful beyond expectations. Through our networks—made up of businesses, professional service providers, agencies, philanthropists, and local volunteers—together with multifaceted in-house services that are all provided free of charge, we've empowered survivors of abuse to attain financial and emotional independence and lasting freedom. For our clients, the outlook had been practically hopeless under the dehumanization of domestic abuse. Now, fulfillment in the pursuit of their dreams keeps them from going back to abusive relationships. Having been empowered to pursue careers they find meaningful, the survivors are now working in well-paid positions, at many employers, including Booz Allen Hamilton, IBM, Macy's, National Geographic.

Second Chance's unique success has been affirmed by no less an authority than the Attorney General of the United States, who presented me with an *Award for Professional Innovation In Victims Services,* in 2007. The U.S. Department of Justice has hired us to train its agents as part of a national crime prevention program. With assistance from government and private entities, Second Chance remains a community-based service. We are also expanding our outreach nationally, and internationally, in the battle against domestic violence and human trafficking.

Our international outreach dramatically expanded in 2009, when the State Department sent me to Syria and Jordan as U.S. Cultural Ambassador on Human Trafficking. In this capacity, I was a delegate for the United States on official missions to countries in Asia, the Middle East, Europe, and South America, where there is a strong interest in finding effective solutions to the epidemics of domestic violence and human trafficking.

In the missions abroad, I have met with high-ranking officials, and dignitaries of foreign governments, and had opportunities to present the Second Chance concept to wider audiences abroad. In May of 2010, I presented the Second Chance model in Geneva to the United Nations High Commissioner for Human Rights. The system has been enthusiastically received. Domestic violence and human trafficking are big problems all over the world. The solutions we've developed here are greatly needed in other countries to stop the human suffering, and to help reduce the economic burdens on society.

Our success would not be possible without the partnerships that Second Chance has formed with those who also have empathy for the survivors. Our partners have said that working with Second Chance is not only personally fulfilling, but also beneficial to their bottom line.

Our dynamic network of agencies, individuals, and private companies includes many types and sizes of entities, from small family-owned businesses, to some of the world's largest corporations. The individuals involved hold a wide variety of political and philosophical viewpoints. (Finding effective ways to combat domestic violence is at least one thing that can attract nonpartisan interest in Washington, D.C. Our services have been engaged and supported by officials in the Bush and Obama administrations and people affiliated with the Republican and Democratic parties around the country.)

Participants in Second Chance's network belong to many ethnic, racial, and religious groups, and diverse economic situations. In addition to partnerships with leaders of many influential companies, we count among our partners and advisors friends from Hollywood and other well known figures, as well as people whose names are not widely known. Regardless of how large or small, famous or unknown, affluent or humble, all join together to help families permanently escape domestic violence and human trafficking.

Second Chance recently formed a strategic alliance with ManPower Group, a Fortune 500 company and one of the largest human resource firms in the world. Our collaboration with them is beginning with pilot locations in the United States, with the potential to expand to any of the eighty-two countries and territories where Manpower Group operates.

As I approached the final stages of writing this book, a monumental advancement has the potential to extend the reach of our system. A new provision in the 1994 Violence Against Women Act ("VAWA") was signed by President Obama on March 7, 2013. This provision makes federal funds available, for the first time in history, to nonprofit organizations that help survivors of domestic violence find employment.

It is a provision I drafted and advocated with the generous *pro bono* support of Jon S. Bouker, partner, and James A. Hunter, Government Relations Director at the Washington, D.C. law firm, Arent Fox. They assisted me in persuading Congress to include the critical funding provision. Our success in getting this provision signed into law will allow financial assistance to other nonprofits that seek to follow our model. The details and significance of this provision is discussed in greater detail in a separate chapter titled "The Second Chance Provision."[4]

This provision had been years in the making. We've demonstrated the tangible benefits of our program both in reducing the enormous costs domestic violence imposes on society, and in the changed lives of survivors, their dependents, and future generations. The new federal funding represents recognition of the wisdom of investing in programs like Second Chance. The costs are justified to improve the lives of individuals now and of those yet unborn, for the betterment of our society as a whole. The investment in a proven, cost-effective program like Second Chance also has the potential to save billions of dollars that are incurred every year in responding to the damages caused by domestic violence.

What started as a small experiment in Washington, DC, has grown to national and international dimensions. There are moments when I step back in wonder at the sequence of events that led us to this point. I'm amazed to see a vision that came to me over a decade ago, something many said was impossible, is now being realized. Its value is being affirmed by prominent leaders in business and government, and most significantly, by the victories of the survivors themselves.

The growth of Second Chance is also a sobering reminder of the scale of domestic violence, the economic and human devastation it causes, and the great task that still lies before us. Today the prevalence of abuse against intimate partners exacts a massive toll on individuals and society.

The National Intimate Partner and Sexual Violence Survey (NISVS) published in December 2011 by the National Center for Disease Control and Prevention ("CDC Report") found, one in four women has been the victim of severe physical violence perpetrated by their husbands or boyfriends.[5] According to the report, "on average, 24 people per minute are victims of rape, physical violence, or stalking by an intimate partner in the United States. Over the course of a year, that equals more than 12 million women and men."[6]

In the clinical terms of the CDC report, domestic violence, "is a serious . . . public health problem that affects millions of Americans."[7] In the conversational tones of the official who oversaw this research, the results are "astounding."[8]

A more sobering assessment still comes from former President Jimmy Carter, in a blog post he recently made. The former president said, "The abuse of women and girls is the most pervasive and unaddressed human rights violation on earth."[9]

Nor is this global scourge predominantly a problem of any particular cultural or economic class. The incidence of domestic violence does not depend on financial position, ethnicity, religion, cultural background, or level of education. It plagues rich and poor, and every strata in between; it is found among people who live in relative obscurity, as well as those who move in circles of influence and power; it affects every sector of society, every geographical region, in America and around world.

The devastation goes beyond the victims themselves. Untold millions suffer harm indirectly by reason of various types of relations to an abused person. The injury is nowhere more devastating than that experienced by the victims' dependents. The trauma to a child who witnesses ritual abuse of a parent causes severe, potentially lifelong emotional pain and suffering. Statistically, they are more likely in adulthood to be victims, and, in some cases, perpetrators of domestic abuse. Also adversely impacted are other family members, friends, co-workers, employers.

Despite the magnitude of the impact on individuals and society, the plague is largely unseen by the public at large. There are various reasons for its invisibility, including the very nature of abuse. Nevertheless, the scale of the plague can be measured in economic terms.

The cost of domestic violence to the U.S. economy is a staggering $8.3 billion.[10] I've been interviewed by members of the press who expressed surprise, even incredulity, at the $8.3 billion figure. In all likelihood, it is understated. It does not take into account many forms of indirect and secondary harm. As I see it, surprise about the enormous costs to society is a gauge of how effectively the daily, tyrannical mistreatment of our fellow citizens is hidden from view.

The economic cost is important but does not begin to describe the human toll. In general terms, the CDC Report hints at the devastation of the lives of millions of individuals: "[m]any survivors of these forms of violence can experience physical injury, mental health consequences such as depression, anxiety, low self-esteem, and suicide attempts, and other health consequences such as gastrointestinal disorders, substance abuse, sexually transmitted diseases, and gynecological or pregnancy complications. These consequences can lead to hospitalization, disability, or death."[11]

Although Second Chance's services include remedial measures for addressing immediate needs, all of our resources are ultimately directed to the goal of preventing future harm. Again, the overarching goal is to empower and equip former victims to live in freedom for the rest of their lives. You could say we are in business to deprive abusers of the opportunity to become repeat offenders.

When victims are temporarily protected and treated for abuse, and then go back to abuse, their misery and suffering multiplies, as do the burdens on society. On the other hand, when a woman permanently leaves an abusive relationship through Second Chance, she becomes financially and emotionally independent. The remedial costs of treating her injuries come to end. Not only is a public burden removed, but there is also an affirmative benefit to society: the former victim's unique talents and interests contribute previously untapped value to her community. In sum, by empowering the former victim to leave the violent relationship forever, Second Chance simultaneously reduces burdens and increases benefits to society—to say nothing of the invaluable blessing of transformed lives of the individuals involved.

The real benefits to individuals and communities are part of the reason why so many leaders in government and businesses actively partner with Second Chance. It is the reason for our success in having the Second Chance Provision passed by both houses of congress and signed into law by the president. Our success attracts people who for a variety of reasons want to see our services help people in their communities, nationwide, and globally. So, the use of our services continues to grow.

While I am encouraged at the success of the enterprise to date, resting on our laurels is not an option! Given the magnitude of the problem, and the millions of victims and their children suffering under domestic violence, in danger of losing their lives by the violent hands of their abusers, our work is just beginning. It is not the growth itself that motivates me. Rather, my passion is making life-long freedom a reality for those who suffer under the tyranny of domestic abuse, human trafficking, and other kinds of oppression.

The same passion that compelled me to found Second Chance—and devote my all to make it work, and expand the reach of its methodology—is what has inspired me to write this book. My hope is to get the word out to expand Second Chance's capacity to help victims; and also to inspire other organizations and individuals to model their approach to domestic violence after the Second Chance method.

With these purposes in view, in this book I am making publicly available for the first time the same information, analysis and advice we were tapped to provide to the U.S. Department of Justice, U.S. Department of State, and other government and private entities. In effect, this is an authoritative primer on understanding and implementing the method of Second Chance.

I hope to avoid a dry recitation of methodology. The aim here is to be not only instructive but also inspirational, to engage both the intellect and the heart. The Second Chance program naturally lends itself to this dual purpose. The principles and practices of Second Chance are inseparable from the dramatic real-life transformations of our clients. So, the true stories of these survivors everywhere inform and are woven into the narrative.

The book consists of two parts. Part One identifies and defines the problem my system was designed to solve—what I sometimes call domestic captivity and disempowerment—distinguishing the diagnosis from popular beliefs, and distinguishing our approach from programs existing at the time I founded Second Chance. Part Two details the practical method we've developed that actually liberates survivors from the invisible prison-camp of violent intimate relationships.

By applying empowerment principles to the problem of domestic violence, and coordinating resources and techniques from a variety of disciplines, the Second Chance solution may represent a new paradigm in responding to this widespread societal ill. For me, all that matters is the system works!

PART ONE

THE CORE PROBLEM:
Domestic Disempowerment

The core problem of a disease is not its symptoms. To find an antidote for a disease, for permanent relief, the underlying cause must be isolated and neutralized. With domestic violence too, I regard the physical and psychological injuries as symptoms. They must be treated and if possible prevented to reduce suffering. My organization, however, plays a different role: to facilitate lifelong freedom for survivors by finding and targeting the underlying cause, the core problem. These pages are dedicated to showing the core problem is domestic captivity. It is a captivity imposed by the gross imbalance of power that keeps victims from permanently ending the violent relationship.

CHAPTER 1

From Inner Void to Inner Voice

"So I returned, and considered all the oppressions that are done under the sun: and behold the tears of such as were oppressed, and they had no comforter; and on the side of their oppressors there was power; but they had no comforter." — Ecclesiastes 4:1

I graduated college aspiring to a career in a field related to my major, international finance. To pursue my dreams, I felt I had to move from my native country in South America to live in the United States.

Then, a tragedy. In 1987, my mother was diagnosed with terminal cancer; and a few months later she was gone. In our last conversation, she said something to me that would have a profound impact on the direction of my life and work. At the time, however, all I knew was the pain of losing her, which was more than I could bear.

She was a beautiful woman of East European descent, having the fine features of a Russian doll, her hair blonde and straight. My mother's beauty was not on the outside only. Her inner beauty could be seen in her compassion for the poor and disadvantaged. Though she had married into an aristocratic class, she helped the poor without a thought for herself. I know of one occasion when she knowingly risked harm to herself to give money to someone in need, and as a result was physically attacked. Though she had no formal higher education, my mother was very wise. Even if she were not my mother, I would adore and admire her and sing her praises.

After she had fallen ill suddenly and was in the hospital with a fever, I stayed with her there. She slept most of the time. While awake, she was weak and not lucid, or at least had trouble putting thoughts into words. One afternoon as I sat alone with her she opened her eyes and took my hand and spoke the words that I would never forget.

"Ludy," she said, "I want you to continue your studies. I want you to work. Even if you marry well, I want you to work. I do not want you to be like me." Her grip on my hand tightened. "Promise me, Ludy," she said. "Promise me you will always work."

With my mind so focused on her illness, my own future seemed hardly worth talking about. Nevertheless, I responded sincerely. "I will," I said. "I promise."

Does it seem strange that the subject of work should be foremost on my mother's mind, even to the point of insisting on this promise? And why did she not want her daughter to be like her? The explanation for these things, in part, is connected to my mother's upbringing. She had grown up in a working class family. The importance of work had been indelibly impressed on her as a child. Her family went through periods of financial difficulty, when any aspirations to higher education and a career had to be subordinated to meeting the present need.

While still a teenager, my mother's fortunes underwent a major change. She married a man from a prominent and affluent family of the aristocracy in South America. It was something like a medieval tale, in which a beautiful working class girl is carried off by the wealthy baron. In reality, in her new life, there was again no compelling reason to aspire to higher education or career, but for different reasons. Now the reason was not financial need, but affluence. Earning an income was unnecessary. And it was a culture in which married women rarely pursued ambitions of their own. As a result, she was financially dependent on my father. She did not seek fulfillment through the use of her other talents, which were considerable.

When she said these things to me about work, my mother knew very well that I intended to pursue a career. She knew I had been accepted to George Washington and Georgetown. She knew that I loved to work. Even as a young girl, I had created and run two little businesses of my own, and earned a profit! So why would she be so passionate about making me promise to keep studying and working?

I believe her words were part of a process of letting go of dreams, and also seeking reassurance that her daughter would have the opportunities she had missed to pursue a vocation, and become financially independent, without having to rely on another. But to understand more fully what inspired my mother's words in those final hours, there's something else you need to know.

In the incident described above, when my mother was physically assaulted for helping a poor man, the one who attacked her was my father. My mother was a victim of violence. She understood what it meant to be trapped and financially dependent on an abusive spouse.

My father, in public, was a paragon of material success, competence, respectability. He was a charismatic, charming man. Behind closed doors he was another kind of person entirely. No one who knew his public persona alone would have believed he was capable of the outrageous abuse he committed against my mother.

Someone once said, "out of deepest wounds, the flower grows." Throughout my formative years, my mother was the source of inspiration and strength. Having her taken from me so suddenly left me deeply despondent, paralyzed by grief for some weeks. It was the sort of grief from which one never fully recovers. But in ways I did not anticipate, my mother's guidance and wisdom, and the promise she elicited from me in her final words, were essential to the solution I would develop years later for people held in secret captivity under a domestic tyranny.

Against the advice of some family members, including my father—who warned that I would be unable to support myself financially—I moved out on my own, before finding a job. For a long time, I struggled with financial hardship rather than return to the financial security of my home. I did so in part to avoid the humiliation of having to admit they were right to say I would never make it on my own.

Someone in my family said I was "crazy" to be going to America to chase some vague dream of "success." I think at some level I viewed that as a challenge to my mother's hopes and expectations, and the promise I had made to her. But I also felt a strong inner sense of a purpose and calling.

I made up my mind to find a job that would allow me to support myself. The experience of facing and overcoming daunting obstacles along the way left me with a deeper empathy for women trapped in domestic violence. Meeting these kinds of challenges helped me develop the solution for survivors of abuse that came to be implemented through Second Chance.

When I first moved to Washington, DC, a friend from my home town invited me to stay with her as I looked for a job. I began my search at embassies and other international organizations, where I felt I had an advantage because of my fluency in several languages. But I had no success at all.

Two days after moving in, my friend told me I could no longer stay with her. She gave no explanation, other than to say that her father would not allow it. It was as if someone were trying to sabotage my plans, and leave me no choice but to return home. One thing was certain. I was out on the streets with my little suitcase and no place to live. To tell you the truth, I was terrified! Of course, I could have returned home. But being alone on the streets and almost out of money was only part of the problem. The option of returning home was tantamount in my mind to giving up on my hopes of financial independence, and breaking my promise to my mother.

I was sitting on a park bench eating a hotdog I'd bought with my dwindling bit of cash from a street vendor. What choice did I have but to return home? What else could I do? Live on the streets? I was on the verge of succumbing to the naysayers. I was almost ready to admit I was wrong. What hope could I have of supporting myself? But I remembered my mother's words. I remembered my promise to her. Again, it seemed to me that to return home would be to let her down.

I wandered around the city until the streets were growing cold and dark, when I came to a small Catholic church. I passed under foreboding gargoyles and through its heavy doors to find it very dark inside. I was frightened and also very tired from hours of walking. After my eyes adjusted, I found a place to lie down on a pew towards the back of the sanctuary, where, using my suitcase for a pillow, praying no one would attack or rob me, I fell asleep.

The next day I showed up at an international organization without an appointment to ask for a job. At the front desk I was told to leave my resume and somebody might be in touch. With a smile and a piece of gum, I persuaded the receptionist to allow me to speak with someone in person. A few moments later, I was telling my story to a kind-faced woman named Coco. She, in turn, took me in to meet the director of human resources. The H.R. director did not offer me a job; but Coco offered me a place to stay, in her home. Her kindness was the only thing that allowed me, for one more night, at least, to avoid the choice I otherwise had to make, between homelessness and giving up on my dreams.

For the next several nights there was a chain of friends, and friends of friends of friends, who allowed me places to stay in their apartments. They were all amazingly kind and hospitable, but as days passed with no success in finding a job, I knew I could not live like this forever. Once again, I began to think I had to give up on my dreams, and return home.

When I'd reached the end of my rope, as a last resort, almost in desperation, I made a phone call to the office of Senator Bob Graham of Florida. He was a friend of my family whom I had seen while staying in Florida a few weeks before I moved to Washington. I spoke to his legislative assistant and asked for an opportunity to meet with the Senator. After meeting with some initial resistance, I hung up the phone with an appointment.

Although I saw the value of my persistence thus far, when I showed up at Senator Graham's office, I had the unshakable sense that this would be my last chance. If Senator Graham was unable to help me find work, it was over. I would have no choice but to return home. Yet I felt confident that the outcome would be positive. Imagine how crestfallen I was, then, when his assistant told me he had "already left."

A few minutes later, standing on a sidewalk near the capitol, I broke down in tears. It was a chilly morning in March 1988. The colorless government buildings were indistinguishable from clouds frosting the sky. I stood waiting to cross the street, brushing away tears and trying to focus my thoughts on what I needed to do to arrange my flight home. When the light changed and I was about to step into the crosswalk, I heard someone call my name. I turned and saw Senator Graham a few yards away walking towards me, waving.

He greeted me, and said how happy he was to have run into me. I was telling him that I had made an appointment to talk about employment when he looked up and called, "Hey, Michael! Good morning!"

A moment later, the Senator was introducing me to Michael Bilirakis, a Congressman from Florida in the U.S. House of Representatives. I told Congressman Bilirakis rather directly that I needed a job. "Come to my office next Wednesday," he replied. So, I did not pack my bags that day. The following Wednesday, I went to see Congressman Bilirakis and he offered me a job as a paid intern.

In the blink of an eye, my whole outlook had changed. I had been desperate to find any position that would allow me to support myself and avoid going back, and now I had a job on Capitol Hill. It was an exciting place to work, and a great opportunity to learn and make professional connections. There was the promise of a practical education in the American political system, possibly even matters relating to international finance.

My early experiences in America shaped the way I thought about helping people in desperate situations. Facing homelessness and poverty with the powerful draw of going back home, where there was financial security but at the cost of my dreams; vulnerability that came with relying on others for help; perseverance in face of daunting obstacles; the value of relationships and networking to finding a job; and the importance of work to financial and psychological independence: in all these ways I had tasted to a lesser degree some of the same kinds of difficulties experienced by those trapped in domestic violence.

In the beginning, I could not have been happier with my job on "the Hill." It was a promising place for any new college graduate to start working. The pay was barely enough to support myself financially, but enough to avoid going back home, and the personal failure that had come to represent.

But the moment of happiness turned out to be short-lived. After a few months of working on the hill, my outlook changed. The great white dome of the capitol rotunda, normally a stirring symbol of American freedom, impressed me then as an empty shell, an outward reflection of the emptiness inside me, a vague longing for something. What the something was, I did not know.

I don't think it occurred to me that it could be related to my job. After all, I had the opportunity of a lifetime, coveted by many young college graduates. I was learning a lot, meeting influential people. But there was no denying it. My initial enthusiasm for the job had waned. In place of that excitement, there was a strange and surprising dissatisfaction.

I was looking for something to do, feeling restless and lonely. One afternoon, after buying lunch in the basement of the Rayburn House Office Building, I was returning to my desk and paused in front of a bulletin board outside our little basement café. Around that time (before the age of smartphones and the Internet in every pocket) I found myself frequently drawn to bulletin boards. I could hardly pass one by without checking to see if anything new had been posted. My preoccupation with the boards could not have escaped the notice of my colleagues. Looking back today, I imagine one of them asking,

"What are you looking for?" To which I might have replied with a laugh: "Honestly, I don't know!"

It was true; I *was* looking for something and had no clue of what it might be. I scanned notices of various shapes and sizes. My eyes fell on a 4×6 card. It read something like this:

> My Sister's Place: Make A Difference
>
> VOLUNTEER
>
> We need volunteers to assist us with programs in our shelter for battered women.

I wrote down the number. Perhaps because I was still grieving the loss of my mother, I felt sad at the thought of children living in a shelter with their mother in distress. I had a desire to help before I'd ever seen them. Within a few days, I was moonlighting as a volunteer at the battered women's shelter that had posted the ad.

The shelter, My Sister's Place, was situated just southeast of the capitol building. To get there, I left the architectural grandeur and important personages milling around the hill, and came to a humble structure in an invisible corner of the city. The atmosphere of the two places could not have been more different. The contrast was so dramatic that they might have been located in different countries, or different eras in history. In fact, they were only a few blocks apart.

There was an equally dramatic change in my outlook and attitude when I was at the shelter. The emptiness I'd felt while focused on my own career vanished when I directed my energy to helping others. Here was the cure for my sense of purposelessness: helping people whose lives had been shattered by abuse; caring for children to allow the women time to go to training for resume-writing and interviewing. Finding work, I thought, would give them a second chance in life.

Being helpful in this kind of environment depended on genuine trusting relationships with the women and their kids. Relationships of this nature would be impossible if one viewed the victim as a stereotype or an impersonal statistic, or in some way of lesser importance because of her circumstances. In my case, that was never a problem. In part because of my close relationship with my mother, who endured that kind of agony, I naturally saw them as unique individuals, created equal in the eyes of God regardless of circumstances.

While helping at the shelter, I had a sense of doing the type of work I was supposed to be doing. I had the peace of knowing I was in the right place, something I did not always have at my paid job. The work was fulfilling. I hardly thought of it as work. I was not looking at the clock to see if it was quitting time. If I looked at the clock it was only with wonder at how quickly the time had passed. I had no objection to staying past the hours I'd signed up for. Without realizing it at the time, I was personally experiencing principles of vocation or calling that were to become indispensable to the innovations of Second Chance.

Before this experience, I'd never heard of a battered women's shelter. I had no idea such places existed. Lenore Walker, author of the well-known 1979 book, *The Battered Woman,* and the subsequent *The Battered Woman Syndrome*, traces the origin of the shelter to England. Specifically, Erin Pizzey opened the first shelter in London in 1972.[12] Soon afterward, shelters were established in the United States and the concept spread to other countries around the world.

What My Sister's Place did (and continues to do today) is incredible. It gives victims and their children a place to live safe from the abusive partner. It also provides food, clothing and other necessary items. It provides training in resume-writing and other skills to help them look for employment. Some of the women told me stories of how they'd been attacked and threatened and had fled their homes with their children, terrified of what would happen to them. My Sister's Place was, in fact, saving lives. Shelters like this, I remember thinking, were a miracle. And they are.

Yet I discovered something else about shelters that troubled me deeply. People I had helped and grown to care for were not leaving the shelter to go on to better lives. Rather, many were going back to the same destructive relationship, the same dwelling, the same life-threatening abuse that had driven them to the shelter in the first place.

I recall with special fondness a family I had helped at the shelter. Two little boys I cared for, while their mother, Linda, was attending training sessions and doing other things to find a job. Linda confided in me about the type of job she would like to find, so she could leave the shelter and support herself and her children. But she spoke of such things with sadness in her eyes, and resignation in her voice, as if convinced she had nothing of value to offer anyone, and therefore no chance of being hired.

My recent struggles looking for a job, as tough as they were, seemed almost a cakewalk in comparison to Linda's plight. She was in a state of paralysis and fear, as if an enemy were closing in on her and her kids as she stood before an austere and insurmountable wall. When she spoke of the type of work she was looking for, she gave the impression of repeating what someone had told her, without conviction. In fact, even the potential to have conviction was missing.

Seeing her in this state, I remember worrying about who would hire her, especially when she herself was sure she had nothing of value to offer. Her mannerisms and appearance, the way she carried herself, showed that she'd been severely traumatized. She spoke in barely audible tones and rarely made eye-contact.

She bore the marks of physical battering—frightful scars; and the purple-yellow discoloration of bruises on her arms. She had nervous ticks. Her natural feminine beauty was hidden behind a veil of diffidence.

All these things obviously put Linda at a huge disadvantage in finding a job. I thought about the services that were being provided to women in the shelter and wondered, how would they be hired for a stable position with adequate pay, absent some kind of miraculous transformation? I tried to bolster Linda's self-image with words of encouragement. But words alone would not effect the kind of sea change needed—any more than resume-writing and other skills, as important as those things are. The wounds of mistreatment were too deep. Dehumanizing abuse had taken a devastating toll.

One evening, when I arrived to volunteer at My Sister's Place, I learned that Linda and her kids had moved out. Assuming she'd found a better place to live, and a source of income, I was overjoyed to think they would no longer have to live in fear of the violent partner. Then I learned she had not found a job or a new place to live. Instead, saying she had "no place to go," Linda had taken her two little boys to live again with the abuser. She'd never suggested to me that going back was even a consideration. Given the emotional bonds I'd formed with Linda and her children, I could not have found words to express my surprise and sadness at the news.

When I started working at the shelter, my assumption was that women came there as an intermediate step along the way to a better life. Eventually, I learned that Linda's actions were not unusual. Many women who left the shelter were taking the same path back to live with the abusers who had been the cause of their coming there in the first place. I'm sure this sad reality weighed on everyone who worked there. At the same time, there was a kind of resignation. It was more or less expected that sooner or later many would go back and that nothing could be done to stop it, unless the victim herself had the will to resist.

But many victims for a host of reasons were seemingly unwilling to separate permanently. In times of extreme danger, they fled to shelters or other places of emergency relief. But often they saw themselves as destined to a life of oppression and abuse, with no hope of escape. Nor were such fatalistic views limited to the victims. It was (and remains today) a widespread belief among lay observers and experts alike. The belief is also shared by abusers, and exploited by them to maintain control over the victims.

The implications of my friend Linda returning to that life were almost too terrible to contemplate. Yet I could not stop thinking about it. The intensity of my emotions over Linda's return did not diminish with time. My heart ached especially for her young children. I knew the desperation of a small child who watches one parent abusing the other, and is powerless to help.

The vivid childhood memories of one volunteer at the shelter contributed to my distress at the news of Linda taking her children back to live in the abusive man's house, where they again would be a captive audience to their father attacking their mother. This volunteer had witnessed violence as a child. Her earliest memories were of her father chasing down and beating her mother. The battering continued throughout her childhood. She never knew when the quiet of her house might be shattered by her father's angry shouts and her mother crying out in pain and terror. It could happen at any hour of the day or night. She remembered the terrible guilt of not coming to her mother's aid, even knowing there was nothing she could do. She would run to her bedroom in a panic and close herself in. There she would hide under her bed sheets for hours.

In addition to the screaming from other parts of the house, she would hear loud banging in the hallways and stairs, knocking and thumping on the walls. She feared he would burst into her bedroom at any moment. But no matter how scared she was for her own life, she felt guilt even as a small child, as if she were to blame for not defending her mother against the vicious attacks. Sometimes the sounds of a violent altercation were so frightening that she would run into the bathroom and lock the door. The poor child would lie on the floor in a fetal position and say, "Oh, Jesus save me!" She would stay there repeating the phrase over and over.

One of this volunteer's most disturbing childhood memories happened at the age of seven, when she witnessed her father perpetrating sickening abuse against her little brother, who was only five. The father beat the little boy with some kind of whip until his back was bleeding. Then he closed him inside a suitcase, and said he was going to throw it into the river with the boy inside. The cumulative trauma of witnessing such atrocities traumatized the girl so severely that for many years she became mute. She continued to suffer severe emotional difficulties throughout her young adulthood.

In the ancient world, seeing the "tears of the oppressed" troubled King Solomon so deeply as to leave him despondent over the value of life itself. Better not to have been born, he exclaims than to see such evil.[13] It is not suffering alone that prompts his life-negating outcry; rather, he says, it is the predicament of those who suffer with "no one to comfort them."[14]

Affliction beyond the reach of a comforter, beyond even the hope of one, also describes the plight of millions in contemporary society who live under the oppression of domestic violence. To witness the dehumanizing atrocities visited on the victims and their children, is to feel an emotional intensity like what is described by Solomon.

This is the dismay I felt as women left the shelter back to go back to the abusers. Even after coming to the shelter for protection, they continued to live in the state of powerlessness seen by Solomon: "on the side of their oppressors there was power; but they had no comforter."

On seeing this I wondered, what purpose have I served? If the women were destined to return to the same household, in the end, what good had all my volunteer work done? Unlike the ancient king, however, my response was not a lament on the vanity of human existence! Rather, for me, the "tears of the oppressed," and the traumatic injury being done to children and their mothers, ignited a passion. The need to find a way to keep these oppressed from returning to domestic violence: this was a burning in my heart.

Almost as troubling as victims returning to their abusers was a prevailing acceptance of the phenomenon, among lay observers and experts alike. Voices all around me were echoing the principle that domestic violence was "an unbreakable cycle"; and that any outside relief was bound to be "temporary."

But I heard another voice too. It was an inner voice, saying, *there has to be a solution!* Weeks went by, then months, and years, and the inner voice never relented or diminished. Finding a solution to the problem of women staying with and returning to their abusers became my calling and my passion. This passion I pursued for years before finally founding the charity devoted specifically to the purpose.

CHAPTER 2

The Direction of Dreams

An Unusual Interview

A young woman of about 25 came to my office without an appointment, looking for a job. My schedule was already filled beyond capacity. There was no way I could interview her on a moment's notice without failing to meet other commitments. But how could I say no? Not so long ago, I had been the one showing up uninvited with resume in hand. The tables now were turned and somehow here I was, on the other side. So, I invited her in and asked her to sit in the chair opposite my desk.

Immediately, something odd caught my attention. There was a noticeable contrast between the boldness of her impromptu visit and certain mannerisms suggesting of an extreme lack of self-assurance. Of course, in a job interview, anyone would be nervous. But this went beyond normal nervousness. The signs of her anxiety struck me as unusual and extreme. When we started talking about some generic job interview topics, an expression of pain, with no connection to the things being discussed, came repeatedly to her face. She had certain nervous ticks, and her fingernails were incessantly digging into the inflamed cuticles of the opposite hand. She hardly made eye contact, but stared at her busy hands, with an occasional furtive glance at the door. She showed the kind of uneasiness that tends to make everyone around her uneasy as well.

Her shoulder-length brown hair had a dry, almost brittle appearance. Her clothes were somewhat worn, not entirely suitable for a job interview at a prestigious firm.

As she spoke in barely audible tones, I considered another contrast. This young woman was attractive, with the kind of lovely features one normally associates with high levels of self-esteem. Yet, she carried herself with the self-abasement of Cinderella, as if she were worthy only of sitting in ashes.

As she struggled to respond to the most basic questions about her background and experience, it was clear that I would not be able to help her find a job. The organization's standards for selecting candidates for employment were well-defined. There was no doubt in my mind that she would be ineligible.

It seemed to me the most compassionate thing to do was to level with her. I decided to share some advice, steps she could take to make herself employable. But when she realized I was not going to consider her for an immediate position, she broke down in tears.

"Please help me," she said. "He's going to kill me!"

It was only now with tears streaming down her face that she finally made eye contact.

I came around the desk to sit beside her. "What do you mean?" I said. "Who is going to kill you?"

"My husband!"

The year was 1994 and I had taken a job as a director of recruitment at a large management consultant firm. It was a bit of a disappointment to me to be working not in international finance, the career I thought I wanted to pursue, but in the human resources department—a field for which I had no particular passion or purpose—or so I thought. But the firm wanted the kind of experience I had gained on Capitol Hill with public affairs, and the job paid well. I hoped working here would afford opportunities for me to transition to the desired work.

I had by now been volunteering at My Sister's Place for several years, and was beginning to take leadership roles in community groups dedicated to helping victims of abuse and other women at risk. I was familiar with statistics on domestic violence, aware of its shocking prevalence. The statistics were roughly the same as today: every year over four million American women are victims of domestic violence; and every day three women in this country are murdered by their husbands or boyfriends. In short, I knew enough to take this woman's fear seriously.

As I grew more active in helping women trapped in these situations, my resolve to find a way to prevent them from going back into harmful situations had grown stronger. In fact, it had become something of an obsession. I was always wondering, what causes them to go back? Could I have said or done something to prevent Linda or other women at the shelter from doing so?

Sitting there with Kara, the young woman in my office, I decided that if I were going to try to help her, I would have to find a way for her to break away from domestic abuse, not for a few weeks or months, but the rest of her life. With that objective in view, I developed a plan. It was a multifaceted plan that addressed Kara's immediate, mid and long-term needs.

She turned her sleeves back to show me marks left by her spouse. Bruises and lacerations covered much of her arms; beneath those injuries were scars from earlier attacks. She told me that he had tortured her by locking her in chains and using cigarettes to burn her arms and stomach.

Staying at the shelter, she saw little if any hope of supporting herself. The abusive spouse had told her repeatedly she could not survive without him. It seemed to me, however, that she could survive *only* without him.

When she tried before to leave him, she'd gone back. This time she was terrified of returning because she was sure she'd "wind up dead."

Eventually, she told me she'd gotten my contact information from My Sister's Place. When she told people there of her desperation to find a job to be able to get away from her husband, my name was brought up because of my position in human resources.

Although she was not ready to be placed in a permanent position, to help prepare her, I took her under my wing, and hired her to work for me as a temporary assistant. At the same time, I was making inquires with a network of friends who were in positions to help with her other various needs.

During Kara's preparation, what I was already learning about human resources and related psychological issues helped me identify and bring out her particular interests and talents. The rediscovery of her personal aspirations, which she had been forced to suppress to avoid triggering a violent attack by her spouse, was not incidental to the process. It was actually the heart of it. At the same time, I was contacting people in my network to find work that both matched her interests and would provide her with financial stability. With Kara's permission, I disclosed to prospective employers that she had been a victim of violence. The challenge was to convince them to give her a chance to prove herself. One of my contacts had an opening for the right kind of work. I helped Kara draft her resume and helped her prepare for the interview. Eventually she was hired.

Henry David Thoreau, recognizing the basic human need to follow a personal calling, offered wisdom on the pursuit of happiness that is at once poetic and practical: ". . . if one advances confidently in the direction of his dreams, and endeavors to live the life which he has imagined, he will meet with a success unexpected in common hours." That is essentially what Kara did. She moved beyond simply clutching for survival and "in the direction of dreams," the life she had imagined. In so doing, she attained independence from the battering spouse, emotionally and financially. The opportunity to pursue her dreams was an important part of lasting financial security. She experienced real empowerment to break the usual pattern of victims returning to the abuser.

As I write today, more than twenty years later, Kara continues to thrive. She remains financially and emotionally independent, and has never returned to the abusive relationship.

Hypotheses and Hurdles

In the context of prevailing views on domestic violence at the time, I knew something exceptional had happened. But was Kara's success an isolated incident? Or could the same method be systematically adapted to help others with similar success? Economic empowerment through the pursuit of dreams I instinctively saw as a universal principle underlying Kara's success. So, I believed the approach used with Kara had potential to help others trapped in violent intimate relationships.

Over the next several years, I was progressing in my career to positions of increasing levels of responsibility, and growing more active in community groups serving women in need. My hope of finding work in the field of international finance had not materialized. Though my earnings increased, I found myself moving further and further away from a career in international finance and more deeply into human resources.

In 1996, I left my job at the management consulting firm to join a non-profit organization specializing in leadership roles for women, where I served until 1999 as Director of Human Resources. All the while I was still looking for work in international finance. From 1999 to 2001, working for a think tank involved in educational issues, I was Vice President of—you guessed it—Human Resources! When I eventually decided to earn a Ph.D., I was persuaded to choose the field of Industrial Psychology—the science of human resources!

Yet, it was largely as a result of my developing expertise in this field that I was equipped to help survivors of domestic abuse. From time to time during this period, women were referred to me from a shelter or church or other organization that helped victims of domestic violence. With these women, I used the same approach that I'd used with Kara, helping them with short-term needs while assessing their career interests and talents, and using a growing network to find suitable prospects for employment. The women I helped, like Kara, were successful in attaining economic independence and separating from the violent partners.

With their successes, my enthusiasm and hope for finding a solution increased. I began to actively plan to launch a formal program of some kind to help survivors.

I was thinking more deliberately then about a new kind of service model. From the beginning, it was concentrated on the single goal: nothing less than permanent emancipation from domestic abuse. The idea was not by any means to replace existing services. Those vital services were treating injuries, protecting victims, and punishing offenders. I envisioned a service that would compliment, and rely on, the services already in place for temporary and emergency relief.

In the early stages, it was almost impossible to get others to share my enthusiasm. Admittedly, the connection between the pursuit of dreams and the mission of keeping survivors from going back to violent relationships was still rather abstract. And as for employment, weren't shelters already offering training in drafting resumes and interviewing? What was so different about my approach? In general, when I tried to explain the differences, I was not taken seriously. Reactions were lukewarm at best. They trivialized my ideas as ill-informed and naive.

In a sense, they may have had a point. I was not at that time reading academic journals or clinical studies on the subject. I was not familiar with a lot of existing research. What I discovered much later is that there was a wealth of empirical evidence that supported my approach; but it was often interpreted through the lens of the prevailing wisdom—including the belief that nothing could be done externally to stop victims from returning to abusers.

What began as a vague idea over time began to take on a more definite shape. I was thinking not in terms of specific academic research or clinical studies. Rather, the steps that had worked with Kara and the others to attain the goal of lasting freedom led me to conceive a special kind of employment service.

My only research to speak of was finding out whether there were, or had ever been, employment agencies designed for victims of domestic violence or others under similar oppression. With the help of my friend, Treva Turner, formerly a director of research at the Library of Congress, I confirmed that there was none. Nothing like this had existed or been tried before.

On the one hand, the lack of precedent was fraught with risk. On the other hand, a new method held the promise of different results—that is, permanent escape from domestic violence.

I began to formulate a nonprofit business plan. Its mission would be to empower survivors through meaningful employment to terminate violent intimate relationships. I was able to conceive of and refine the approach in large part based on the expertise I'd been developing in my capacity as a consultant and manager for sophisticated firms, doing the work I'd tried to avoid—namely, human resources. One of the things I'd seen through that experience was the importance of assessing talents and matching them to dreams and aspirations. For women whose dreams had been crushed by abuse and whose talents forced into dormancy, the element of individual "calling" was of critical importance.

It was human resources combined with my experience as a volunteer for women at risk that afforded insight to techniques for discovering and developing talents and passions of such women. After assessing talents and interests, the next step was to find the place where those talents would be used to contribute value and earn a fair return. With Kara, my prototype, a network of prospective employers was instrumental in making this step a reality.

Obstacles, in the form of personal opposition of friends and colleagues became so difficult that at times I was prepared to give up the whole idea. This was especially intense after I mentioned the possibility of quitting my paying job to form the non-profit company. My husband Joe, at that time was just starting his career and our daughter

Megan was a little girl. Why would I think of leaving a well-paying job to spend my time working for a non-profit business, doing something never before tried that could generate no income?

Much of the criticism seemed anything but constructive. For example, I heard: "you want to leave your well-paying job to devote yourself to finding jobs for people no one will hire?" One person who prided herself on being forthright and direct, said, "You're crazy!" Unbalanced by positive suggestions, some of the objections seemed to be opposition for opposition's sake.

Friends, family, professional acquaintances, and others I genuinely respected, were strongly against my taking steps towards a solution for survivors of abuse. Nothing is more valuable to me than personal relationships with people I care for. Now, a number of those relationships seemed to be strained to the breaking point, all because of my vision. The whole business was almost unbearable.

Some of the criticisms were to be expected. Well-meaning friends thought it would be unwise to quit my job, and give up the career I'd worked so hard to advance. I had finally gotten to the point where I was financially independent. Why would I just throw it away? Why not just continue along the current track—as a volunteer in my off-hours for various service projects; and as a paid consultant at my current firm?

Another intense reaction came in the form of arguments against the substance of my plan. To some critics, the concepts were strange and counterintuitive. I was proposing a system that went against what they had learned about victim behavior and the "cycle of violence."

At the risk of oversimplification, this kind of criticism can be distilled as follows: unless and until the victim came to a decision on her own to terminate the violent relationship permanently, no outside help would induce her to do so. It was up to the victim. If she were unwilling to leave the abuser, all my efforts to help her do so would be futile. Unless her desire to leave was stronger than her reasons for wanting to stay, efforts to help her terminate the abusive relationship would never work. I think someone pointed out that if she developed this strong desire to leave permanently, the kind of service I had in mind would be unnecessary.

The nearly unanimous negative reaction to my ideas was obviously discouraging. It gave rise to a kind of inertia that I now think must have been mild in comparison to the paralysis of victims who contemplate ending a violent intimate partnership.

But in the end, I knew the reason for pursuing the vision was not about me. It was to help these oppressed people and their dependents, who were suffering so badly with no hope of escape. So what if these personal criticisms and negative responses hurt my feelings?

Also, I knew they were wrong. In my heart, I never believed that a person stayed in violent relationships because of a lack of will to leave. It was always my conviction that the victims were powerless to leave. Kara's success served as a ringing confirmation of my intuitive ideas. The skeptical responses, though discouraging, could not dissuade me from trying to help others using the same method.

Thoughts like these were like a gold thread leading to my goal. I clung to the thread, even when I did not see precisely where it would lead.

Another obstacle I encountered was the lack of time. In my consulting and managerial work, I was working extensive hours, traveling around the country. I had almost no time to focus on the volunteer work. Certainly I lacked the time required to launch a new business. I knew that in order for this experiment to have a chance, I'd have to quit my job and devote myself to it full-time.

Before taking that step I had to have others to join with me in the venture. Indispensable to Kara's success were the people who were empathetic to her plight and willing to help in some aspect of her restoration. The entire system would depend on a collaboration of like-minded people. So, my business model called for a network of partners.

Very few people were willing to join me in pursuing the vision. To persuade people to make an ongoing commitment of time, effort and financial resources in something out of step with conventional approaches seemed all but impossible at times, especially in the absence of supporting scientific studies or empirical evidence. However, there was no getting around it. Before quitting my job to form a non-profit business, I would have to have a group of people willing to pledge their support.

The Law of Innovation

When just about everyone else seemed opposed to me, I met with a very kind man, the rector of a church, who prayed for me, and gave me wise advice. He talked about what was required of someone who had a vision and a desire to make that vision a reality. For any vision, no matter how large or seemingly insignificant, one requirement was this: you must step into the unknown. Resistance to innovation was inevitable. It was an immutable law. There may be many reasons for resistance, but it often comes from people who have your interests at heart but who see only what is, and not your vision of what could be. So, you have to step forward by faith.

I suppose it was only fitting that I too should be challenged in this way to "advance confidently" in the direction of my dreams. With this perspective, it was also apparent that I did not have to choose between my vision and my respect for those who opposed me. Many who tried to dissuade me from carrying out my plan were trying to help. Some were affirmatively trying to protect me from a course in which they saw no prospect of success.

After this meeting, I redoubled my efforts to find partners. Stepping forward in faith, with renewed confidence in the direction of my dreams, I think I became more persuasive. A small but growing number found my approach interesting enough to pledge informally to support the project in various capacities. Over time, with perseverance, I had a total of 40 commitments from business leaders, service providers and others to support Second Chance in various capacities.

Now I was prepared to take the next step into the unknown. But could I really quit my job, and give up my career to start a non-profit company?

In addition to the pledges of 40 partners and the clergy who prayed for me, the indispensable source of support was my husband. Without his support and willingness to take the risks involved in the endeavor, Second Chance would never have happened.

The Founding and Fulfillment of Promise

In December of 2001, nearly seven years after the Kara's liberation, I quit my job to start the charitable organization, Second Chance Employment Services.

The mission of the business was to institute an antidote to the problem of women staying with, and returning to, violent relationships with intimate partners. I did not form it based on abstract theories or academic research. It was based on the practical steps I'd taken in collaboration with friends and professionals who shared my compassion for the victims and were in a position to help. To some extent, the steps were intuitive common-sense responses to physical, emotional and financial oppression, under which I saw the victims trapped.

I came to understand that what I had regarded as a hindrance was actually preparation for realizing my vision. My jobs in human resources were all necessary steps along the way. Through this experience I can also lend perspective to my clients by helping them consider how something that may seem out of sync with their goals is actually a step towards meeting them.

It occurs to me also that my mother's advice to "always work" was all about, yes, human resources! But, what about my promise to her? After promising her that I would always work, here I was, quitting my job to devote myself to launching a charity with no earning potential. Was I breaking my promise? No, to the contrary, I see the decision to institute Second Chance as the perfect fulfillment of my promise, and consistent with my mother's wish for me.

My work would be to help others work. In this enterprise, two things my mother loved, charity and work came together. For this reason alone I think she would have loved the idea. What about her concern with my independence? I decided that if it was meant to be, everything needed to make the business work would fall into place. And it has. But there is more to freedom and independence than money. With my experiment to do the work I felt called to do, to help people in dire need, I had the sense of personal fulfillment. And, for independence that is true and lasting, it is essential that work be meaningful. This principle is an important aspect of the success of Second Chance.

CHAPTER 3

Why She Stays . . . And Why We Ask

W*hy does she stay?* It must be among the most frequently asked questions about domestic violence—perhaps second to, *Why would she go back?* Another is, *What attracted her to such an abusive person to begin with?* These questions are practically unavoidable in conversations about domestic violence. They have been for decades a topic of intense interest in academic and scientific studies. They are questions that were raised in the very first book published in the United States on the subject of domestic violence, Del Martin's groundbreaking 1976 book, *Battered Wives,* published by Volcano Press.

In 1989, in an article, "Helping to End the Assaultive Relationship," P. Lynn McDonald pondered what she called the "intellectual puzzle" of why abused women have trouble ending violent relationships. The article cites numerous other articles that had already considered the question at that time.[15]

In answering the question *Why does she stay?* there is a common thread of belief that the victim bears some part of the responsibility for her own predicament. In their excellent book, *It Could Happen to Anyone: Why Battered Women Stay*, Ola W. Barnett and Alyce LaViolette summarized a number of earlier studies showing "public opinion about battered women":

> A 1987 survey of 216 randomly selected respondents revealed that more than 60 percent agreed that if a battered woman were really afraid, she would "simply leave." Over 40 percent said the victim was "at least partly to blame for her husband's assaults" when presented with a story that provided no factual basis for the conclusion. There was also tendency for respondents to believe that the woman must have been "masochistic or emotionally disturbed" if she stayed and that victims "could avoid the beatings if she entered counseling."...[16]

Based on these studies, the authors conclude that popular beliefs about domestic violence "rest upon widely held and false assumptions." The studies are useful in documenting popular confusion about victim staying behavior. This is not to say that asking the question, and even coming up with the wrong answers, necessarily indicate an unfair prejudice against victims of domestic violence. The questions may also be motivated by reasonable and good intentions to make sense of observed facts and to determine the best way to help those in need.

How can we be sure the beliefs described are "false"? Is it possible some of the widely held views are correct? Why should we accept the woman's account as true? Isn't it possible that she bears some of the blame for her circumstances?

As implied in Barnett and LaViolette's book, some incorrect popular opinions may not be false assumptions so much as misinterpretations flowing from an incomplete understanding of the facts. The beliefs, though wrong, need not be attributed to prejudice against battered women. They may be rational observations based on observed behavior.

Why does she stay? Before answering the question, it is worth thinking about another: Why do we ask? What makes it so important? Professor McDonald noted, that our understanding the reasons why victims don't leave their abusers "has implications for the interventions and the services required to facilitate the process" of helping them end the relationships.[17] Indeed, the way we, as individuals and as a society, answer the question of why victims would stay with abusers clearly impacts our response to the scourge of domestic violence. It affects our willingness to help; it affects the form such help will take; and it affects the underlying purposes of offering help.

For example, a program designed to help victims escape permanently is harder to promote as a worthwhile endeavor if the victim herself is deemed somehow responsible or unwilling to exit the violent relationship. With this point of view, other types of services may still be seen as fully justified to remedy an acute attack—e.g., medical and legal assistance to the victim; shelters and other protective services; punishment of offenders by the criminal justice system; and perhaps psychological counseling or other intervention to help prevent future violence. But if the victim has decided to stay of her own free will, why devote significant resources to help her leave? That action would be the victim's to take.

Another factor in the latter case is concern for privacy. Efforts to help victims leave intimate relationships might be seen as an intrusion on the personal choices of consenting adults. No matter how terrible the situation may look from the outside, if the victim continues to live with the offender, resources devoted to talking her out of it may do more harm than good. Regardless of credibility or moral accountability, if the victims themselves are unwilling to leave, devising a system to persuade her otherwise would seem an exercise in futility. Compassionate people who hold this view may conclude that their charitable impulses are best directed elsewhere.

The significance of the *"why does she stay?"* question, and the critical need to get the answer right were dramatically illustrated in the trial of Barbara Sheehan in the fall of 2011. Ms. Sheehan was a victim of domestic violence who was thrust into the national spotlight when she was tried for the second degree murder of her abuser, her husband, Raymond Sheehan.

Although Ms. Sheehan admitted to shooting him multiple times at close range as he stood shaving, to the charge of murder she pled not guilty. Her plea was based on what is commonly known as the "battered-woman defense." For over twenty years, Mr. Sheehan had terrorized his spouse with atrocious physical and psychological abuse. During the Sheehan trial, the jury heard detailed evidence of the brutality of the slain man, including testimony of the Sheehan's two grown children. His physical violence against Ms. Sheehan included throwing a pot of boiling liquid at her, smashing her head against a cement wall, punching her in the face, pointing a gun at her, threatening to kill her. Mr. Sheehan's son, who had witnessed the physical and verbal of abuse of his mother from a very early age, testified that his father was "a monster." According to Ms. Sheehan's testimony, the threats against her life had intensified in the weeks, days and hours leading up to the shooting.

Notwithstanding such heinous criminal conduct, the prosecution argued, people are not permitted to take the law into their own hands. In theory, there was nothing to stop Ms. Sheehan from escaping the danger posed by her husband by leaving the house and calling for help. The fact that she did not leave was evidence that the testimony about the existence or severity of abuse was false. Thus, the *"why-would-she-stay?"* question loomed large in the Sheehan case.

As the trial was proceeding, before the jury returned a verdict, a nationally syndicated radio host expressed his misgivings about the battered-spouse defense. The commentary lends an articulate voice to popular and longstanding views about victim staying behavior, and is therefore worth considering. The commentary was verbatim as follows:

> .... If someone were beating me up, and abusing me, I would get out of there. I would call the police. Especially in this case, where he was threatening the

children, there is no way I would stay in that relationship. So, I have to ask, *why did she stay* with him all those years?

And it seems from the reports here that a few weeks before she killed him, she went away on vacation with him to a tropical island. And she had gone on many vacations with him before that. And now I have to ask, how can she assert the battered-wife's defense? Why would she go on vacation with him? *Why would she stay with him? Why did she not get out for her own sake and for her children if he was such a threat to her life?*[18]

It seems to me the question, *Why did she stay?* is driven by two other unstated questions. First, *is she telling the truth?* And second, if she's telling the truth, *is she partially to blame?*

In the absence of another explanation for why she stays, it may be reasonable to wonder whether she's telling the truth about the existence or severity of the abuse. For one who has never experienced or witnessed domestic violence, the idea of her staying in the wake of such atrocious mistreatment might well seem contrary to strong survival instincts, and to a parent's protective role.

As Marjorie Bard wrote in 1994, "[v]ictims of abuse have an added burden: few people believe that any woman in her right mind would stay with a man who beats her."[19] Ironically, the victim's worrying about such reactions to her staying becomes an element of her paralysis that keeps her from even trying to escape.

The commentator quoted above expressly indicated that his view was based on his own personal experiences. It was his experience and observations in life that led him to believe Ms. Sheehan must have had innumerable opportunities over the years to separate from her husband, up to and including the very morning of the fatal shooting. Yet he later acknowledged that he had never been victim of domestic violence or witnessed it. Again, from a subjective point of view, his questions are not unreasonable, maybe even unavoidable, in a serious evaluation of her defense.

In public debate over the trial, others expressed the opinion that allowing the battered spouse defense was unjust in the Sheehan case. Though I strongly disagree with that conclusion, I do not think it's fair to attribute it to prejudicial ideas about Ms. Sheehan, or false assumptions about victims of domestic violence generally. Rather, like opinions I hear often from people with the best intentions, the commentary on the victim's failure to leave comes from an incomplete understanding of domestic violence, its tyrannical nature, and its dehumanizing effects.

The prosecution in the case likewise questioned Ms. Sheehan's credibility. Appealing to the jury's common sense and common experience, the reasoning of the argument went something like this: with abuse as severe as she claims, the defendant would have left; she did not leave; therefore, the abuse must not have been so bad, if it occurred at all. Ms. Sheehan claimed that his conduct was so violent that her life depended on killing him. Yet, she did not take the obvious, non-violent survival measure—namely, according to the prosecution, leaving him. Moreover, life insurance proceeds and escaping justice would have motivated Ms. Sheehan to make up or exaggerate the severity of the abuse. It's hard to deny the argument is persuasive.

Another question within *Why does she stay?*, has to do with principles of freedom and responsibility. If Ms. Sheehan is telling the truth about the severity of physical and psychological abuse, then shouldn't she be accountable for the consequences of her decision to stay? In a free society, we believe personal freedom is inseparable from personal responsibility. If we're free to make choices about intimate relationships, then we must be responsible for those choices.

Notably, the surveys cited above indicate that no one thinks a victim's decision to stay makes the batterer any less blameworthy for his crimes. The moral principle involved, however, is that a person generally does not gain the right to take the law into his or her own hands by choosing to stay in harm's way. So, if her life was in danger, and she could get out, Ms. Sheehan had a *duty* to get out —to remove herself and her children from the threat. Here again, the idea is valid and should not be lightly dismissed as stemming from ignorance or unfair prejudice.

Although the Sheehan case may help illustrate the reasons why we ask the question, up to now, it seems we've made no progress in actually finding the answer. But the outcome of the case points us in the right direction. For in spite of the powerful arguments offered by the prosecution, and the subjective life experiences of the jury, the jury found Ms. Sheehan had indeed acted in self-defense. On the charge of murder, therefore, it returned a verdict of not guilty.[20]

The arguments against Ms. Sheehan implicitly required the jury to evaluate widespread beliefs about the victim's staying behavior like those offered by the radio commentator. The not guilty verdict suggests the jury found those explanations wanting.

Now, the Sheehan trial did not require an express answer to our question, "why did she stay?" But I don't see how the jury could avoid deciding whether her failure to terminate the relationship proved she was lying about the abuse. And I think the jury also had to decide whether staying with her husband meant she could have no reasonable expectation of imminent harm to herself when she pulled the trigger. Certainly the verdict in her favor means the facts gave the jury reason to believe Ms. Sheehan's account. And they must have had reason to believe the abuse occurred with such severity as to traumatize Ms. Sheehan, to make her fear for her life, and reasonably believe that she was threatened with serious physical injury or death.

If members of the jury had believed Ms. Sheehan was to blame for not leaving, would they have reached the same verdict? I don't think so. The verdict of not guilty suggests a rejection of the attempt to blame her for staying in the relationship. Even so, does the verdict have any significance beyond the specific facts of the Sheehan case? There are reasons to think it does.

Because domestic violence is mostly hidden from public view, perceptions of victim behavior may be based on subjective experience, gossip, something read in a novel, seen in a movie or on TV, or on other popular misconceptions. These misconceptions are made without direct knowledge of the victim's experiences or the degree of control exerted by a violently abusive person.

But the jury is exercising a solemn duty to determine the truth of the matter, based on eyewitness accounts, given under oath, all tested in the crucible of a criminal trial. In this controlled environment, the Sheehan jury would have seen a re-creation of the experiences of the victim. To evaluate her defense, justice demanded that they have a clearer view, and a deeper understanding, of what such a life is like.

And what did they see? The brutality, the oppression and the atrocity, in all of its disturbing detail, that ordinarily cannot be imagined by someone who hasn't lived through it or witnessed it. It cannot be imagined by someone who hasn't lived through it, or witnessed it. The importance of their own subjective life-experiences about what they would do under such circumstances could only be diminished, if not entirely eliminated from the equation.

Still, we may wonder, are the facts of that trial specific to the Sheehan situation? While every individual, and every intimate relationship, is unique, we know the "staying" behavior is a constant. This whole discussion is premised on the theory that the phenomenon has universal attributes and common causes.

The Sheehan decision supports two general principles. First, staying in the relationship does not automatically mean the victim is exaggerating or lying about the severity of the abuse. Second, a victim who stays with the abuser should not be presumed responsible for her circumstances or her own injuries.

The Sheehan verdict and others like it, give us strong grounds to doubt certain popular ideas about victims' staying behavior. To succeed in my mission, I had to do more than rule out wrong answers. I had to find the right one. My passion to find a lasting solution was also from the beginning linked to a need to understand the reason why so many women at the shelter were going back to the abusive households.

The innovations of the Second Chance system, and our track-record of success, are a product of the answer we've adopted.

My approach departs from popular beliefs about victim behavior like those reflected in the commentary on the Sheehan case. If I had accepted those as a starting point, Second Chance would not have made its goal permanently ending domestic abuse. Again, I've always rejected the idea that the victim makes a free-will decision to stay in or go back to the abusive relationship. So at Second Chance we exclude from consideration the role of some hidden desire or willfulness on the part of the victim to stay and be beaten and terrorized; we focus instead on empowering her to leave.

I should emphasize that my approach does not come from naiveté about victims of violence, or from regarding them as models of perfection who never make mistakes or do anything wrong. The victims are as prone to err as anyone else, and, like everyone, have unique strengths and weaknesses. The challenges they face are intensified as a result of years of recurring assaults and cruel psychological oppression. In looking at what prevents the termination of violent relationships, the victim's shortcomings are *not* in my experience a core problem that needs to be addressed. It is neither a lack of desire nor motivation on her part, nor a moral deficiency that causes her to stay.

As tempting as it can be to conclude otherwise, personal flaws are not, in any relevant sense, the reason why she stays.

Why does she stay? Despite appearances to the contrary, the decision to stay is not a decision at all. She stays because she lacks the power to leave. In the end, my answer to the question may be distilled to these two words: *domestic captivity.*

CHAPTER 4

Contrary Theories

It is not just the general public who has erroneous ideas about violent intimate partnerships. A widely held view by experts, found in various theoretical approaches to domestic violence, is that, before they can escape, the victims must first have a change of heart. They must decide of their own free will to terminate the relationship. Before they take that step, it is thought that there is no hope of helping them escape permanently.

My own belief is that the desire and the will to leave already exist. The problem is that it has been coerced by violence and other means into dormancy. This may seem like a small or subtle difference. But in terms of finding ways to assist survivors of abuse, it is huge.

I did not know it at the time, but prevailing theories in academic and scientific papers were at odds with the beliefs that formed the approach I would take. Some popular theories relating to the issue are referred to as the "cycle of violence," "learned helplessness," "codependency," and "traumatic bonding."

the relationship to be as it was. This may be another way of saying that she needs to come to her senses.

Similarly, those who embrace "learned helplessness," "traumatic bonding," "codependency," and the like, to varying degrees emphasize the need for victims to become emotionally independent of the abuser. Here the problem is seen as a need to wait for the victim to change her mind and will, perhaps with help from counseling, about wanting to remain with the abuser. From this perspective too, services would tend to focus on providing temporary relief for the immediate pain and suffering.

Regardless of which theory, or which combination of theories, one might find persuasive, there is invariably a belief that unless and until the victim develops the will to terminate the relationship, there is no way to stop her from returning. Before she comes to that point, services for battered women are there to provide temporary relief.

But this was the very problem I had witnessed and was determined to address. I saw victims leaving shelters to return to heinous physical and emotional abuse. I witnessed small children having to again experience the unimaginable pain of witnessing one parent's brutality against the other. And I was remembering that every day in America three women are murdered by their intimate partners, so she may not survive through the next cycle.

While volunteering at the shelter, it never occurred to me that women who had fled for their lives from vicious attackers might go back to the attacker three to five times before they could hope to end the relationship. I could not tolerate the idea of a woman returning once! It's not that anyone else found the popular theory tolerable. But I sensed a general belief that it was tragically inevitable; that nothing could be done to change it; that any attempts to do so would cause more harm than good.

I saw it differently. A woman who fled for her life to the shelter did not need to go back and forth until circumstances forced her to make a decision. Rather, she was paralyzed. She was standing terrified on the edge of a dark spiraling vortex of overwhelming power, drawing her back into the black hole of injury and death. I wanted to find a way to get her out of that whirlpool to some solid ground where she could stand, so that she and her children would not be forced back to that place of pain and despair.

This is why a major part of Second Chance gives shelters and others to whom victims flee a place to refer the survivor. At Second Chance we take hold of people standing within the reach of the vortex, even as the Alaskan native American takes in a wounded eagle. The Second Chance program then empowers the survivor to rise above the spiraling whirlpool on her own strength.

Why was there such resistance to a solution to patterns that everyone found unacceptable? The popular conventional thinking, as well as prevailing expert theories about victim behavior, fueled resistance to the solutions I was proposing. It was believed that nothing could be done unless and until the woman came to a decisive point where she wanted to leave the abuser, more than she wanted to stay. There was the mindset that resources are limited, and must not be spent on exercises in futility. All efforts should be concentrated on the immediate needs of those hurt by domestic violence: medical, psychological, legal and survival needs were viewed as paramount.

This is not in any way to diminish the vital importance of those services. It would be impossible to overstate my regard for the amazing and miraculous work of those who aid victims of domestic violence, who treat their injuries, provide for their safety and protection, and help them survive in innumerable ways. Their work is absolutely indispensable.

Yet, those measures alone are not designed to facilitate a permanent transformation. So, while my program for permanent escape would include partnerships with existing services, it also meant going against the current of prevailing concepts to develop another kind of service.

Based on my volunteer work with women at the shelter, I knew they wanted to leave. It was not a problem of will, but of power. The success of Kara and others left me with a mission to prove that any survivor could be empowered as they had been, to break the cycle of violence, without going back to the abuser.

Social activists tend to agree with me that the solution has little if anything to do with changing the victim's heart or mind. They emphasize the need to continue to work for structural and cultural changes to rectify gender inequality. Their legal reforms and other activities over the course of many decades have already done much to rectify imbalances in power between men and women. I have no doubt that continued progress on that front will reduce the frequency of domestic violence. In the meantime, there are millions of victims today, suffering real atrocities at the hands of violent intimate partners, without hope of escaping. So, Second Chance works on a different front, within the existing cultural norms, to facilitate personal and financial empowerment, one woman at a time, as a lasting solution to domestic violence.

CHAPTER 5

Domestic Captivity

To isolate and bring into focus the specific problem Second Chance was formed to solve, I've introduced the term domestic captivity. As used in this book, domestic captivity refers to the condition of a person who has been deprived of power to terminate an abusive, violent intimate relationship. It does not mean captivity in a particular physical location, though physical confinement may be involved.

In general, the strength of domestic captivity builds over time. Captivity is accomplished by the cumulative impact of overlapping abusive behaviors. Abusive behaviors include physical violence, psychological abuse, verbal abuse, economic abuse, and others.

From the outside, domestic captivity is mostly invisible. There may or may not be signs of abuse. The relationship appears to be voluntary, and thus the victim (if perceived as such), is thought unwilling to end it. The outward appearance thus contributes to beliefs that victims have decided of their own volition to stay in the relationship. But with domestic captivity, appearance is by no means reality. The victims are powerless to leave.

A state of domestic captivity exists not only when the victim is physically present within the domicile shared in common with the abuser; it continues so long as the victim is emotionally, financially, and in other ways, locked in a relationship with the batterer. If it has a shape, domestic captivity is best understood as the kind of vortex described in the previous chapter. So, it continues when the victim is physically not within the domicile but remains subject to the gravitational pull of the abuser's dominion. Whether at work, on vacation, or staying temporarily at a shelter or with relatives, the victim remains in domestic captivity as long as she lacks power to end the relationship permanently.

Domestic captivity is accomplished in increments. It occurs gradually, over time, by a series of abuses. There are degrees of restraint that progress towards full captivity. How does one know if a state of domestic captivity has been imposed? Based on the experiences of my clients at Second Chance, if, after one instance of physical violence, however seemingly minor, the victim does not immediately terminate the relationship, she is already in captivity. But the reality of disempowerment typically is not understood by the victims; or if there is awareness it comes only gradually and sporadically. Certain elements that combine to prevent and forestall detection are themselves an integral part of disempowerment.

The assertion that women are literally trapped in domestic violence may be hard to believe. Women who remain in abusive relationships are seen in public. They may have a job and a car of their own. They show up at battered women's shelters, hospitals, and courts. The resources of federal, state and local governments exist to protect people from domestic violence and punish offenders. How, then, can it be said victims of violence are powerless to leave?

In trying to understand someone else's circumstances, we naturally begin with what can be observed, and measure those observations against our own experience. So, another reason for doubting domestic captivity is personal experience. We saw an example of this in the radio host's comments about the Sheehan trial: "If someone were beating me up, and abusing me," he said, "I would get out of there. I would call the police." He later went on to say that he had never witnessed, or been a victim of domestic violence. His assessment of the victim's behavior began and ended with his own experience.

Most people have never experienced, witnessed, or perhaps even imagined being violently abused by an intimate partner, let alone held captive in their own house. But we know that what goes on behind closed doors in violent households differs dramatically from our own experience. It follows that our own subjective experience should not be relied on, at least not exclusively, as a basis for evaluating or interpreting the victim's behavior in staying.

Instead of personal experience, I recommend viewing the victim's actions or inactions by looking at alternative models or allegorical comparisons. The idea of the vortex provides one such comparison. None of the more elaborate models described below is a perfect analogy; but each helps to show from a different vantage certain aspects of the victim's predicament.

The Maximum Security Prison

Let's take what will seem an extreme, even unworkable, comparison. Imagine a woman is literally a prisoner in her own home. Though her residence may from a distance resemble a normal house, on closer examination we find it is a maximum security prison. Picture bars across every window, steel-reinforced doors with sophisticated, impenetrable locks, and high walls all around the perimeter, topped with barbed wire and shards of glass. The perimeter is protected by electronic surveillance systems and loud sirens in the event of an unauthorized exit. There are strategically placed turrets at every corner, behind which armed guards are stationed. Imagine this woman is held in this prison unjustly, without having committed a crime. And suppose that within the prison, she is habitually beaten and in other ways abused. She wants nothing more than to escape. But seeing any effort to escape would be futile, she makes no attempt to leave.

No one would say such a captive suffers from lack of will to leave, or harbors some hidden desire to be beaten and abused. No one would deem her morally responsible for staying there. Words to the effect that "she has only herself to blame" would not be whispered by outside observers. We would not trouble ourselves with unfair prejudice or theories about victim-blaming. As helpful and interesting as the theories may be, ideas about "learned helplessness," "traumatic bonding," "cycles of violence," and "codependency," would have no application here. If the victim is physically imprisoned, it is clearly understood that it is not about her will or moral probity. It is, rather, about power. It is clearly understood that the prisoner's power, her freedom to leave, has been taken by the one who imprisons.

This comparison invites an obvious objection. Domestic violence typically does not involve physical incarceration. It occurs in the context of an intimate, consensual relationship. Indeed, the image of a maximum security prison stands in contrast to a seemingly obvious aspect of victims' failure to terminate abusive relationships: namely, they stay not by reason of any steel bars but their own their own free will, their own decision.

Yet the parallel between incarceration and domestic violence is closer than first appears. Almost without exception, there is a powerful unseen mechanism that holds the victim captive. Though invisible, it is a captivity every bit as real as physical bars. Just as in the case of a physical prison, the victim of domestic violence stays not out of any lack of desire to be free, but rather the lack of power. A multitude of abuses, of which physical violence is only one, is the cruel mechanism by which the victim is disempowered and paralyzed. The cumulative effect of abuse serves as a steel latticework that keeps her from walking, and, at critical times, from even trying to walk, away.

And why is this unseen confinement of domestic violence invisible? To be effective at all, the curtailment of the victim's freedoms must be kept secret. If the confinement were detected by others, it would not be tolerated. False imprisonment, after all, is a criminal offense. This leads me to a second allegory.

Invisible Fence And Shocks

I have a friend whose neighborhood regulations prohibit the residents from erecting new fences and from using cables to prevent their dogs from leaving their property. His neighbor has a dog that was fond of bolting out of the door, across the front yard, and through the neighborhood. Other neighbors complained. After receiving a written warning from the housing association, the neighbor found a solution: an invisible electric fence.

The electric fence is made by transmitters installed underground around the perimeter of the property. A special collar put on the dog administers a shock whenever he approaches the property line. He is thus confined by his aversion to the shock, to the area delineated by the invisible electric field. Like a bird in a cage, he does not even try to leave.

If you did not know about the invisible fences, it would be reasonable to think this dog could take off anytime he wanted to. And seeing he makes no effort to leave, you might easily assume he's perfectly content to stay in his yard.

In reality, he would prefer very much to escape. So the truth of the matter is quite at odds with what we see with our own eyes. Just remove the collar, or power off the transmitters, and show him there's no longer an electric shock at the border: and off he goes! He is running through the neighborhood again, just like the good old days.

As long as the device is active, the dog stays in the yard. Nothing could entice him to leave. He would not leave to chase a rabbit. He probably wouldn't leave for a T-bone steak. Trying to change his will has no effect because without any enticement, his desire to leave is already very powerful. In other words, his staying is not a problem of the will; it is a problem of his power (or perceived power). To set him free, we'd have to solve the power problem. And to solve the power problem, we'd need to know about it in the first place. We'd need to know about the invisible mechanism that holds him captive.

With domestic violence, there's also an unseen barrier, yet it is every bit as real and effective as a physical cage. Like the invisible fence, it is unnoticed by everyone but the one it is intended to control. The means of her confinement are hidden. We don't suspect the many forms of abuse working under the surface to render her powerless to leave. So, we easily assume she stays with the abuser of her own free will.

The Bird Cage

A third allegory has already been introduced in the Prologue. The wildlife rescue serves as a kind of parable, of loss of power followed by empowerment. For purposes here, though, I wish to emphasize the captivity phase. The wounded eagle was not grounded by any lack of will to fly. Rather, it had lost the power of its wings. Of course, the loss of ability indirectly softens the will to escape. Put another way, the loss of ability can make the will go dormant. But this is quite different from saying that a weak will is the reason the animal stays. No, it is the loss of power that weakens the will . . . not the other way around.

In the film sequence described, we see the eagle when its desire for freedom has come back to full strength, beautifully resilient. Why does that desire, that will, come back? Because its strength has returned. The moment native power is restored, the will to escape revives. With health and strength restored, the cage is opened, the eagle is released, and it flies off at once, uncontainable. The image is powerful for me because it represents the experience of many victims of domestic violence who became clients of Second Chance.

Again, a caged bird, even one that has not been injured, will not ordinarily try to escape. Could anyone think the lack of effort means the bird is content with its cage? Of course not. If it is impossible to fly, then it is madness to try. Equally erroneous, though maybe not obviously so, at first, is the idea that staying with a domestic abuser is a sign of the victim's contentment or willingness to stay.

In the case of domestic violence, the "cage" is unseen. But if an invisible cage renders escape impossible, such captivity enervates the will no less than a physical cage. To anyone who observes the captive not

CHAPTER 6

Domestic Tyranny

Under certain totalitarian regimes, vast populations suffer in ways that may be hard for people in a free society to imagine. Only rarely do the subjects of a brutal dictatorship try to leave. Yet no one asks, "Why do they stay?" No one wonders whether they remain out of some secret desire to spend their days in misery. Nor would we suggest that the oppressed are to blame for their predicament.

Imagine asking the citizens of the former Soviet Union why they failed to terminate their citizenship and just leave the country. Or suggesting since North Koreans rarely escape their country, the despotic ruler must not be so bad. Or that victims of Saddam Hussein's reign of terror who could not escape had only themselves to blame if they were tortured. To raise, in this context, the questions asked of women who do not get out of domestic violence is ludicrous.

If we were persuaded that conditions under domestic violence are analogous to those under a political tyranny, then some of the popular beliefs we've seen about domestic violence victims might be recognized as equally absurd.

It turns out there are striking parallels between the two forms of tyranny. In fact, they are nearly identical in both the means of oppression (types of abuse) and the impact (disempowerment) on individual victims. Whether oppression comes from a political body or a personal relationship, from the position of the oppressed, it is devastating. In both, there exists a grotesque imbalance of power, where the subject or victim is disempowered; and in both the disempowerment allows the oppressor to hold the subjects in captivity.

The similarities between public and private tyrannies are anything but superficial. Illuminating the similarities may help dispel shadows lingering over the question of why victims of domestic violence stay with abusers. To crystallize the connection, I use the term domestic tyranny.[24]

Many distinctions could be drawn, between a tyranny of the state and domestic tyranny. Most of the differences are a matter of scale, not of kind. Notably, in both types of tyranny, the victims stay for the same underlying reason. Before a variety of intermediate causes, there is a common first cause: it is the lack of power to leave. Tyranny in government and tyranny in the home both work a systematic dehumanization of the victims that deprives them of the power to leave.

People living under the control of a cruel dictator do not stay, ultimately, of their own volition; they live under varying degrees of compulsion and constraint, moving towards, if not already secured in, complete captivity. Captivity under an oppressive government tends to be accomplished by a combination of military, financial, and psychological control. The "iron curtain," a term popularized by Winston Churchill in a 1946 speech, described the isolation and control imposed by the Soviet Union. The term remains a somber image of tyranny today. Churchill's primary reference was the military force (the "iron") that had amassed along the borders of East Europe to prevent emigration. The "curtain" was an allusion to efforts to keep the people from seeing life beyond the borders. As such, it contributed to the regime's "arbitrary control upon the thoughts of men," to quote Churchill on his broader observation on tyranny. In addition to physically contain-

breaking off an abusive relationship, when the force holding her there is unseen, it's easy to assume her lack of power is actually a lack of desire or will.

We might hear observers say something like this: "she stays because she has no desire to leave." In reality, she shows no desire because she has no power to leave. My strong view of powerlessness in certain ways conflicts with theories about victim behavior previously discussed. It is this conflicting perspective that accounts for the innovative methods developed through Second Chance.

....

The maximum security prison, the bird cage, the invisible fence, and other comparisons, are intended to guide us to a truer understanding of the core problem. One thing I hope they help illuminate is the role of disempowerment, as distinguished from a lack of will or desire of the victims, in the mystery of why they stay.

Metaphors have limitations, and can take us only so far in illustrating domestic captivity. If an electric fence or a jailhouse were a perfect comparison, then leaving the domicile to take temporary refuge in a shelter would not be an option. An important difference is that domestic captivity is not imposed exclusively, or even primarily, by physical force; nor does it in most cases confine the victim to a physical area. Yet there is another model of comparison with parallels to domestic captivity that are closer and less abstract.

ing the inhabitants and controlling their vision and thoughts, the iron curtain was also an image of the autocratic government's veiling from the outside world the appalling mistreatment of its people.

In our contemporary world, the state of citizens under tyrannical control is occasionally glimpsed by citizens of the free world. Recently, Sophie Schmidt, the teenage daughter of Google chairman Eric Schmidt, after accompanying her father to North Korea, made some revealing observations: [25]

> Our trip was a mixture of highly-staged encounters, tightly-orchestrated viewings and what seemed like genuine human moments . . . .We had zero interactions with non-state-approved North Koreans and were never far from our two minders. [26]

She described the room to which they were conducted to witness the supposedly modern state of internet usage. What was intended as an exposition of a tech-savvy populace, Ms. Schmidt recognized as a facade:

> A few scrolled or clicked, but the rest just stared. More disturbing: when our group walked in…not one of them looked up from their desks. Not a head-turn, no eye contact, no reaction to stimuli. They might as well have been figurines.

The description of the people resembles the demeanor of victims of domestic violence I've observed over the years. Among the traits that cue me in to the possibility of domestic abuse is a woman's avoidance of eye-contact. Like the North Korean subjects, victims sit silently, diffident, in compliance with the abuser's wishes, even when the abuser is not physically present. They have learned the arbitrary nature of his retribution. They know the most innocent utterance, a look or a gesture, may trigger a violent attack. The safest course is to remain silent (though even silence may trigger an attack).

An iron curtain of sorts descends around households in the grip of domestic violence. The physical brutality and threats of violence might be thought of as "iron," while various non-physical abuses are a curtain contributing to the control and containment of the victim, limiting her ability to see beyond the tyrant's dominion, while precluding knowledge and intervention from outside by a shroud of secrecy. The veiling of atrocities that go on in the secret shadows of domestic tyranny helps to explain the persistent misinterpretations of victim behavior, and the mistaking of a victim's powerlessness as a personal choice to stay in the relationship.

Domestic violence is a genuine tyranny. Although the oppression is perpetrated against a single individual, rather than a whole nation—for the victim, the suffering is every bit as real. Millions of victims of violence in America, and scores of millions around the world, collectively make up an entire nation under tyranny. As with the subjects of a despotic government, subjects of domestic tyranny share the same core predicament as citizens under state despotism. Disempowered by the oppressor, they are powerless to leave.

CHAPTER 7

True Stories of Domestic Captivity

Diane: From Rags to Riches to Rags

She speaks with such clarity and eloquence that if she told you she'd won first place in a state-wide speech contest, you would not be surprised. Nor would it surprise you to learn that in high school, she'd been elected vice president of the student counsel, or homecoming queen. In fact, Diane had done all these things.

What might surprise you, however, is that this now-successful business woman was once a victim of domestic violence. She suffered heinous physical and psychological abuse at the hands of the man she married, and remained in captivity for twelve years under a tyranny of his brutality. Several times she had fled from him to save her life, and each time went back to live with him again. Diane was finally referred to me at Second Chance Employment Services. The happy outcome of her restoration and permanent escape is told in Part Two. But here her life in the violent relationship illustrates real-life domestic captivity.

Yet she never thought of his criticism as unfair or excessive. Rather, due to the incremental aspect of its intensity, she continued to think he had her best interests at heart. Thanks to him, she was only being made aware of something she'd never noticed: a defect in her manner of communicating.

With many years of psychological battering, this champion of a state-wide speech competition grew insecure about supposed "defects" in her speech. She felt uneasy about expressing herself in his presence, in the company of his friends and family. The intimidation made her more likely to falter, and faltering would tend to give rise to additional criticisms. Lowering self-esteem affected all of her relationships, even inhibiting interactions with her childhood friends and family, who had always known her as confident and carefree. She was only vaguely conscious of the gradual change in her attitude towards herself; nor, again, did she recognize his behavior as abusive.

In addition to knocking down her self-worth, and sabotaging her identity, the verbal abuse in Diane's case was a direct attack on her freedom of expression, a first step in the subjugation that would grow into domestic tyranny.

"Every day," she says, "he would find some imperfection or inadequacy. He would go on for hours about something I said or did." What had begun as "constructive criticism," was more and more manifesting itself as anger. She recalls the disturbing incident when this anger exploded into a terrifying menace: "He got mad at me about something when he was driving the car. He screamed he was going to drive into a tree and kill us both."

There followed a period of relative quiet. Weeks passed without incident. He was once again treating her with seeming affection. She began to think of his display of murderous rage as an isolated incident. With the passage of time, and continued "romantic" treatment, she was convinced she'd exaggerated the severity of his conduct in her own mind, that she was "just being paranoid." It must have been stress that had caused him to act that way. And if she had been more careful not to upset and provoke him, the whole incident would have been avoided.

Eventually, there was a second outburst of similar intensity and terror, then a third. In each instance, his rage was all out of proportion to whatever she had said or done to trigger it. And he was always implacable:

> There was nothing I could say to calm him. Anything I said would only make him angrier. If I said nothing, he'd be mad about that. If I expressed agreement with him, he'd accuse me of trying to appease him.

Much of Diane's mental life was now preoccupied with how to avoid upsetting him. "I never knew what might trigger his anger," she recalls. As his "anger became more intense," the abuse moved from being exclusively verbal criticisms and threats to physical violence against property. "He started throwing things and breaking things."

Like many victims of domestic tyranny, Diane was greatly unsettled by the unpredictability. There was the sense of "always walking on eggshells." In fact, it was not eggshells, but her life that was at risk.

Though seemingly arbitrary—his vacillating from one extreme to the other, and the disconnect between her actions and his reactions—increased his power over her. This development was another step in the gradual progression from initial entrapment on the way to complete domestic captivity.

The process of taking control of her life is especially clear from his economic abuse, whereby he coerced her to stop pursuing a career and acquiring resources.

> Anytime I wanted to improve my career he would always say, "I have the stressful job; you should have the easier job; take care of the [house]." I took a couple of classes at college and . . . he said he was getting robbed . . . of the relationship. [T]he whole idea of me taking the class . . . that was one of the times that he really got violent.

She recalls a disturbing incident that seemed to be unrelated to economic abuse.

> [He] was driving the car and I was in the passenger seat. I made a grammatical error, and he exploded in anger. He became so furious that he punched the windshield and broke it with his fist.

You might think such ugly abuses would be a powerful incentive for a person to get out once and for all. Yes it would be, if the same menacing act did not also strengthen his control and limit her freedom to think independently. In this one outburst she was subject to multiple abuses—verbal, psychological, economic. Together, they magnified his control in several respects. The wildly disproportionate and alarming reaction to her supposed linguistic error was a drastic suppression of her power to speak freely.

The episode is an example of how physical, emotional and economic abuses combine to hold the victim captive. It was a few days before the windshield incident that he had told her to drop out of college. The demand naturally upset her. He was asking her to give up something she'd dreamed of doing from a young age. She had already reduced her studies to one class per semester. A direct conflict (artificially imposed by the abuser) between two strong desires of her heart tormented her unspeakably. She wanted more free time to devote to improving their marriage. For her the marital relationship was sacred. To make it better she thought there should be no limit to one's willingness to sacrifice. Yet she was still passionate about pursuing her childhood dreams of higher education and career.

A few days after the windshield incident, she dropped out of college. His menacing behavior had shaken her to the core. More so than ever before, she was afraid of making him angry. "I just wanted to keep the peace, so I didn't continue with my education."

But coercing her was more than fear of physical harm. Her power to think independently had been undermined by the combination of abuses. She describes her thinking at the time.

> The shattered glass was my fault, he said. And I agreed. I mean, I didn't just say I agreed. I believed him. . . . Then he said it was my responsibility to have the windshield fixed. So I did. I made all the arrangements to replace the broken windshield.

Her belief that she was responsible for his misdeed shows the damage done by the years of psychological abuse. In addition to severely eroding her confidence and self-esteem, he had assumed a degree of control over her thoughts and beliefs that is characteristic of domestic captivity. She dared not question her abuser's pretense to infallibility. If he said she was to blame, it must be so. So, it was only fair for her to have to fix it.

Although there was no mention of her college courses in the conversation leading up to his outburst, there was no avoiding the direct connection between the two things. "When I tried to finish the class, that's when he broke the [car] window." Even so, she saw her own shortcomings as the cause. She had not immediately dropped the course, and continued attending the class, even though she saw how it was upsetting him. His mood had darkened as his verbal battering became more frequent and intense in the days before he punched the windshield. If she had not been so selfish, she thought at the time, he would not have reacted so strongly to her failure to speak correctly.

As she now understands, the possibility of her earning a college degree, with its potential to enhance her financial independence, threatened his domestic domination and captivity. The use of wild, irrational rage as a coercive tactic to interfere with a victim's acquisition of resources is a classic form of economic abuse. "That is what punching the glass was about," Diane explains. "He wanted me to depend on him financially. And I did." Thus, in addition to verbal, psychological, and physical abuse, his violence against their property amounted to significant economic abuse.

Inseparable from this economic abuse was the way it undermined a major source of individual power. By this, I mean her dreams. The possibility of fulfilling them had grown increasingly remote. Now the dramatic escalation of abuse further disempowered her not only by blocking the acquisition of resources but also by removing from her the right to pursue happiness.

Diane's description of the events shows the erosion of her personal freedom and power:

> I was unaware of how much I had changed. If he had told me not to go to college in the very beginning, I would have doubted him. But now instead I doubted my own thoughts and plans if they conflicted with his. ... When you hear something over and over you begin to believe it. . . . I had a lot of respect for his intelligence. If he said a career was wrong for me, he must be right. So I gave up trying to get a degree.

He had exploited her trust to his own advantage. Her ideals of selfless love in marriage he twisted by coercion to the notion that by pursuing a college degree she was putting her own interests over his, and over their marital relationship. Under this latest menace, she only hoped that trusting his judgment and conforming to his will would help him to "get better," and their relationship would return to its former fairy tale quality.

In addition to repressing self-worth, the incremental abuses were wreaking havoc on her perceptions, undermining her thought processes. If, at the beginning of the relationship he had berated and menaced her, she would not have tolerated it; much less would she have thought herself to blame. She would have ended the relationship. But her disempowerment and captivity came with the cumulative impact of gradually increasing abuses. His creeping tyranny was more and more controlling her thoughts and emotions. Even before the onslaught of physical brutality, he had diminished her power to leave the relationship.

"Through all this, I never thought of myself as being abused." Again, in keeping with what her husband was telling her, she believed she was mostly to blame for his abusive behavior.

"I mean ... it becomes a type of brainwashing where you feel responsible for their actions. Maybe not everyone. But like in the beginning, I felt responsible for him acting that way."

Convincing her that she was the cause of the abuse was another aspect of his ability to control and hold her captive.

In the first three years of their marriage, this manipulation of her thoughts and emotions had been done without physical violence against her person. But now the removal of the freedom to pursue a degree and her aspirations marked a turning point. By bullying her to drop the college course, her prospects for financial independence and personal fulfillment were shoved out of sight, below the horizon. This level of domination was a signal that her captivity was now secure enough to contain her, even in response to physical attacks.

Diane's husband had been a college athlete, over six feet tall with a muscular build. During the early years of their relationship, when he presented himself as the embodiment of good manners and grace, his size and physical strength impressed her as a source of security and protection. Little did she imagine that these same qualities would become a threat to her own life, that his powerful hands would be used mercilessly and repeatedly as weapons against her.

One morning she was violently yanked out bed and woke to find herself flying across the bedroom. She smashed headfirst into the wall and fell to the floor with her legs twisted beneath her like a pretzel, making it difficult to move.

> I was lying on the floor and he was screaming at the top of his lungs. I was frozen there for I don't know how long and I couldn't move and I really didn't even

> know what was happening. It was like a dream, only there was this burning pain in my head from the impact. Then he started pulling everything out of the closet in a frenzy and throwing stuff at me. It took me a minute to figure out what had set him off. What he was yelling about was, when he got out of the shower and dried himself, some fuzzy stuff from the new towels I'd bought stuck to his skin. It was my fault he said because the towels were brand new and I hadn't washed them. When he was finished ripping apart the closet, he said I'd have to put it all back, before he got home from work. And after he left, that is what I did. When he said I was to blame, I believed him, again. It didn't matter that we just moved to that house, and the washer and dryer weren't hooked up yet.

The attack on her as she slept was the beginning of years of routine assault and battery. "The violence escalated," she says. "It became so bad that I got restraining orders. He violated the orders and was arrested a couple of times." There were intervals of calm, lasting days or weeks, sometimes months.

Then the attacks resumed without warning, often without a discernible cause. With physical battering, he inflicted crushing physical pain. He also crushed her spirit.

> He began doing horrible things. Once he got upset when he was leaving for work, because he couldn't find a tie or something. And he spit in my face.

More than once, he tried to strangle her.

> One time he had a belt around my neck and was going to strangle me with it because we were going to visit his mother and I was running late.

In that instance, he was so furious, she thought he was going to kill her. But just before he tightened the belt to cut off her breath, she said, "think about what your mother would say." At that point he turned and walked away.

Before the physical violence, she says, "I was afraid to express my ideas, because I thought they were wrong." After the physical attacks on her person, there was obviously a new dimension to her fear. "I was afraid of what he might do to me. . . I was scared to death to say or do anything that might trigger his anger." It was an anger like nothing she'd seen or experienced in any other relationship—a wild, uncontrollable fury, "explosive and unpredictable."

> Then he would say things to me like he was going to light me on fire and throw me down the steps. He would describe how he was going to throw lighter fluid on me and light me and throw me down the steps. He said things like that.

She lived in mortal dread of her own husband.

The inexorable question we've examined at some length—*why would she stay*—perplexes no one more than the victim herself. Diane explains her thoughts and perceptions living under full-blown domestic tyranny.

> Why on earth did I stay with him? Why didn't I just leave? I've thought about that question a lot. . . . I believed I was completely dependent on him. This was a huge factor. [He] kept me from getting a job. He became very angry if I said anything about resuming college courses. When it became intolerable, and I actually wondered if I should leave him, he said that if I ever left I would never be able to take care of myself. It seems crazy, but at the time, I was sure he was right. It was a great fear.

The same fear is expressed by people living under despotic governments. A strong deterrent to leaving their country is the fear they would not survive without their ruler's providence. The fear is inculcated by years of propaganda; it is pressed into their souls through hardship, by the autocratic ruler's control of material resources. If the choice is either to survive without freedom or to risk one's life, and the lives one's children, just to wind up in poverty, it is no choice at all.

Diane's husband's business had been growing and thriving and became very lucrative. They were living well, as measured by material wealth. They moved to a large house in an affluent, gated community, with luxuries beyond anything she had known.

There's a common perception that domestic violence is something that happens to the poor and poorly educated people. In fact, the frequency of the crime does not vary by income or education. The forms of oppression and obstacles to freedom may be different; but not the degree of pain and suffering.

Diane's husband's fortunes and growing influence in his line of business emboldened him to exert greater control over her and further restrict her freedom. The increased income, praise of peers, and power over employees invested him with an aura of superiority and authority. If his pronouncements at home had been authoritative before, now they were infallible. Banished was any lingering doubt about who was best-suited to be the "breadwinner." His surging prosperity was now used to validate his assertion that she had no need for a career. The opulence of their home and furnishings, and all the luxuries and privileges that came with wealth: these became constant tangible reminders of his superiority and power. Greater wealth and influence allowed him to build on the insecurities he had been fostering in her from the beginning, and that now became a major factor in her captivity.

The human needs for security and meaning in Diane's married life were increasingly tied to a sense of belonging to her spouse's professional and academic society. "As if I could acquire those things vicariously," she reflects, "and so become more acceptable—a worthy person." At the time she did not think of how he exploited these universal longings by fraud to entrap her, and to hold her captive by abuse. The messages spoken and unspoken were consistently that she had no hope, no identity, and no worth outside the relationship with him. Thus, instead of providing security and meaning, the abuser used his power to deprive her of both. He had induced her to depend on false security and false significance. As in a government tyranny, neither physical force alone, nor the threat of it, kept her from escaping. The verbal, economic and physical abuses combined to allow him to gain control over her mind and spirit, and build ever higher walls to keep her from leaving.

In addition to the psychological components of economic abuse, his material wealth also generated a physical environment conducive to captivity. The sheer size of the house; the acres separating it from other residences; the gated community and its private streets; the exclusivity and privacy of clubs—all served to set her dangerously apart from family, friends and communities of aid and support.

Thus, instead of providing more freedom to pursue happiness, her husband's prosperity led to greater isolation and a more austere captivity. Like many violent intimate partners, he blocked her access to bank accounts and other resources. She was not free to spend money without his permission. Despite having every modern convenience, she lived more like a medieval damsel in distress, imprisoned in a dark tower. The one who held her there was the very person who had presented himself fraudulently as a "prince in shining armor." In fact, he was more like the *Prince* in Machiavelli's famous book of that name, a ruthless dictator with an insatiable desire to control his subject.

With gradual acclimation to the abusive environment, pain and loss of personal freedom was the norm. She came to see dependence on him as an unchangeable fact of life. While taking control over income and assets, he coerced her with abusive tactics to believe she had nothing of value to offer, that she had no capacity to survive without his financial support. These ideas he conveyed through years of abusive words and deeds and she was hard pressed to believe anything different.

He threatened to harm her physically and financially if she ever tried to divorce him. He vowed to hire the most powerful attorneys money could buy to ensure she would be left with nothing. He said no one would believe her stories about abuse. Given common misperceptions about victims of domestic violence, this was a real possibility. She feared that trying to leave him would result in physical harm and economic destitution. He told her, and she greatly feared that if she left she would wind up homeless.

False ideas about her own inadequacy to earn an income, and the exclusivity of his providence, went beyond financial security. "I felt dependent on [him] for just about everything. For love and acceptance. For my own identity. For my purpose in life." She no longer dared to dream the dreams that once motivated her. Now routine abuse of utmost cruelty had made her numb to all the things that used to motivate and inspire her.

She tells of an episode that shows in a dramatic light the extent of her powerlessness:

> I remember one of the times he tried to strangle me, on a winter night. I got away from him, and ran out into the snow in bare feet. We lived on a hill with a few acres, and I ran barefoot in the snow all the way to a neighbor's house. The police came and ... they arrested him. They wanted to prosecute him. But the state had to drop the case because I decided not to testify.

This was not the first time Diane chose not to pursue remedies available under the legal system. In the instances he was arrested for violating protective orders, she says, "I didn't press charges."

How can it be said she was powerless when the power of the state was ready and willing to prosecute him for felony offenses? The answer lies in the very decision not to pursue the legal remedy. In that decision we may see an important facet of disempowerment and domestic captivity.

> By this time, I recognized that [he] had problems. But my only desire was for him to get better. I prayed so hard that he would get help. . . . Even though I had to get restraining orders to protect myself, I thought if [my husband] only got help, we could still have a happy life together. So, I didn't press charges. I wouldn't testify. I had this hope that everything would work out. I also had a terrible fear of losing him. And I remember thinking that if he went to jail things would be even worse when he got out. I mean, he would kill me.

Thus, the structure of her captivity included the overlapping bars of fear and hope. The hope that she could help him "get better" is a classic element of domestic captivity. She was distressed by the state of her marriage, which could not have been more different from what she'd imagined as a child. She'd grown up anticipating the sort of happy relationship she had seen between her parents.

From the beginning, he had preyed on her hopes and expectations. He exploited her ideals of selfless love, and solemn intent to keep the wedding vows. He took advantage of her respect and admiration for him, and her trusting nature. He had followed a path seen in many abusers, identifying vulnerabilities, disguising his own abusive nature in chivalry and generosity to ensnare her.

After an acute attack, her husband's flattery and professions of remorse and undying love bolstered her hopes of his "getting better." The hope of returning to (what she regarded as) their former bliss was not something she had power to pursue, much less make happen.

> What I know now is that domestic abuse only gets worse with time. The longer you stay in, the worse it gets. The one being abused has no power to cure the abuser. The only way to survive is to get out.

The predicament, however, is that she also has no power to get out.

might get better with time. That he would change, and she herself could be the instrument of his cure.
- **Guilt, Shame.** He had coerced her into believing she was to blame for problems in the relationship and for his mistreatment of her. He exploited misperceptions of society to convince her that no one would believe her if she complained about abuse. The imagined shame of being considered a failure as a wife kept her from reaching out for help, and contributed to her isolation.

There are innumerable manifestations of this sort of captivity in the experiences of Second Chance clients. Some variations are evident in Myra's narrative that follows.

Myra: Exploitation of a Mother's Love

In the beginning, Myra's spouse was outwardly a model of gentleness and respect. Within a relatively short period of time after their marriage, she saw his personality changing. He became brusque and irritable and his interactions with her were marked by a severity she'd not seen before. While still newlywed, she allowed herself to believe the changes were part of a normal process of adjusting to life together; so she was not greatly troubled.

Before meeting her husband she had worked as an accountant. At the time they married, she expected to continue to pursue a career after marriage. They planned to have children, and she agreed that when the time came she would suspend her career to stay home while the children were young. Upon the birth of the first of three children, she quit her job. It was then that he began to abuse her.

After expressing his preference that she stay home to raise the child, he verbally berated her for having no income. The woman he formerly said was the "love of his life" he now called a "leech" and "a liability." He began to control the domestic finances, with a control that gradually tightened over time. He occasionally threatened to harm her physically if she acted contrary to his will, with special emphasis on her use of money. Once, during an argument while their first child was still a toddler, he shoved her. A few weeks after that, he began striking her. With each successive child, the abuse grew more frequent and more severe.

Pregnancy and giving birth are widely understood as triggers of domestic violence. Many of my clients at Second Chance were victims of this barbaric pattern. Though such heartless crimes are ultimately inexplicable, the phenomenon fits with my identification of the core problems as disempowerment and captivity. Pregnancy and giving birth is often a time of heightened vulnerability, when a woman may be naturally inclined to look to her partner for support and protection, and generally to depend on him more than at other times. In non-abusive relationships, of course, a father of an expected or newborn child tends to be especially supportive and protective. A mark of the abusive person, however, is to exploit vulnerabilities to gain control.

Myra's experiences provide a disturbing illustration. Her maternal devotion to the newborn baby; conflicting obligations of career and motherhood; postpartum depression, and other physiological conditions following labor and delivery: all these circumstances the abuser took advantage of to enhance his control and strengthen the captivity. She lacked an income. So, he insisted, her access to financial resources must be curtailed. At the same time, he dampened her expectations of returning to work outside the home. He trivialized all her dreams and aspirations. Through verbal, physical, and economic abuse, he demoralized her, wore down her sense of identity and worth, and increasingly controlled her life.

Her unemployment was the pretense he relied on most heavily to justify his assumption of control over money and all other resources. He appropriated all assets to himself by putting titles and accounts exclusively in his name. He cut off her of access to cash by cancelling her credit and bank cards. In the end, she literally had to beg for money to buy necessary items, such as food and clothing for herself and the child.

While her absence from the workplace extended over a period of years, she lived under degrading subjugation at home. Gradually, unconsciously, she acquiesced to his characterization of her as a non-contributing burden, devoid of value, lacking any capacity to earn an income on her own. Such perceptions evoked feelings of guilt, shame, and lack of self-worth, which also facilitated his ability to control her.

Despite her efforts to mollify him and avoid doing or saying anything that might provoke his anger, his physical attacks became more savage and dangerous. After one particularly brutal assault, in response to her spending money on basic items, she resolved not to spend money on herself. But, of course, the attacks continued.

As the cumulative impact of his various abuses sabotaged her identity and self-worth, thoughts of professional aspirations and dreams became very remote. In this way, her suffering was magnified by the oppression of purposelessness.

Many of the same elements that kept Diane from leaving her situation worked to entrap and imprison Myra as well. Like Diane, she often fell into longing that her spouse would somehow revert to the person she'd known in the early years of their relationship. With the birth of the third child, when his mistreatment became so abominable as to be truly unbearable, she could no longer suppress the reality that she was a victim of domestic violence. However, under the full measure of the tyranny he had built, she felt that she was powerless to leave.

We may wonder about the impact of a mother's natural desire to protect her children. Wouldn't maternal impulses have given her a strong compulsion to escape? As often happens, Myra's abuser manipulated her circumstances to use those same maternal impulses to fortify her captivity. He told her that if she left, he would take custody of the children. Her years of unemployment, lack of income, and conduct showed her emotional instability, and her unfitness to be a parent. By repeating messages of this nature, he convinced her to accept the idea that if she left him she would lose custody of the children. The strong desire to protect her children was twisted into an incentive to stay in the relationship. Given his demonstrated willingness to carry out the most vicious of threats, it was plausible that the only way to stay with her children was to stay with the husband. Her maternal instinct to protect her children became the heavy bars of her prison. At the very least, it neutralized the simultaneous drive to separate based on that same protective impulse.

He also browbeat her with the common misperceptions about domestic violence. If she'd really been treated so badly, he said, why would she have stayed all this time? If she told anyone she was being abused, who would believe her? If she and the children were in danger, why didn't she leave? The reality of the misperceptions, and the shadows they would cast on her, was another element of her paralysis. The more time that passed, the greater the doubts against her would be, and the stronger their deterrent effect. In this way, the "why would she stay" question becomes a "Catch 22"—another bar of the prison of domestic captivity.

Separation seemed certain to lead to a worse situation than even the present. Down that road, she saw only abject poverty. So, even if she managed to win custody of her children, she would be leading them to material deprivation and homelessness.

Regardless of what might be said of cycles of violence, or the number of attacks that often occur before a victim will leave the abuser, the lack of power to end the relationship may go on indefinitely. In reality, many victims are ultimately killed by the abuser. For others, a breaking point may come first. Though they have been deprived of the power to end the relationship, there may come a point where they actually lack power to stay.

To put this scenario into the allegory of the invisible dog fence, imagine that a ferocious lion enters the scene. At that point, the dread of the electric field gives way to another dread. The dog dashes out, right through the electric shock. This sort of situation helps explain what happens when a woman flees to a shelter. Unlike the dog, however, she remains subject to the control of the abuser even after she has fled.

One day, when Myra's youngest child was seriously ill, his fever spiked, and her husband refused to allow her to take him to the doctor. He would not give her any money, or transportation, and told her that without a co-pay, the doctor would refuse to see the boy. She did not really believe a doctor would refuse to see him, but she was afraid to question his statement. As she watched her pale little boy go limp and fade in and out of consciousness, her increasingly desperate pleas were met with increasingly angry refusals. There came a moment where she knew that if she asked again, he would beat her. She feared he would kill her, or at least render her physically incapable of helping the boy.

The abuser's extreme indifference to the boy's well-being and prohibition of taking him to the doctor was cruel in the extreme and truly evidenced a murderous intent. Through all the physical and psychological torment he'd visited on her, such a depth of his depravity she'd never seen. Standing before her now, punishing her by keeping her from getting help for the boy, was a monster. The threat was akin to that of a ferocious beast poised to take the life of her little boy.

She felt like a woman imprisoned in a high tower, holding her son, when the tower was suddenly engulfed in flames. Under his tyranny, she had no power to escape the relationship. But with this impending destruction, with the choice between death by immolation and death by falling, what could she do? Myra did the equivalent of the latter; leaping into what she thought would be her demise. In desperation she took the boy in her arms and ran out of the door.

Thankfully, it was not her demise. Myra survived the escape. On the night she fled, she found a doctor for her son, by asking a neighbor to help. Of course, on seeing the limp child shivering in his mother's arms, the last thing on the doctor's mind was a co-pay. That this did not occur to her before is a classic example of the abusive spouse's control over the victim's thought-processes. Myra found a shelter; and from there she was referred to Second Chance. The rest of her story is told in Chapter 16.

Like Diana, Myra entered into marriage with high expectations. Her abuser's false representations during their courtship and engagement concealed his despotic designs. The relationship she believed she entered actually never existed. The actual relationship, full of terror and abuse, was nothing like the one she reasonably expected based on his representations. The violently abusive relationship in which she became ensnared was never voluntary.

Lucy

What follows is a paraphrased translation of the account of a survivor of domestic captivity whose native language is not English.

I left [my country] to marry a man who promised to love, honor and cherish me as his wife. He promised also that I would have a better life as a citizen of the United States. I believed this man was telling the truth. For me, it was like a dream come true. But after I arrived, I discovered he had no intention of marrying me. He had deceived me into coming here to become, in essence, his slave, over whom he would have power to isolate and abuse, with no one to intervene. By the time I fully understood his intentions, I found myself already trapped in an abusive relationship, believing was no way out, no hope of a better life.

Instead of making me his life-long partner in matrimony, this man made me his unpaid housekeeper and the caretaker of his children. I had to perform many demeaning tasks. I was abused physically, verbally and emotionally. In the isolation of a small rural town in Virginia, he subjected me to horrible things that no human being should have to go through.

He threatened me so I would not leave. He took advantage of me as a foreign person unfamiliar with American laws and culture. I felt completely dependent on him for everything, especially financial security. He said I could not survive without him. I believed him. I felt there was no escape. After [we] had a son, he used the child to keep me from leaving. Many times he said he was going to call INS and have my son taken away. I was scared I would lose my son. It was overwhelming. I lived in fear, and I had no hope.

cases are rape and other heinous sexual assaults, which may be classified as a separate form of abuse.

Physical violence results in the victim's death with greater frequency than is generally known. In 2010, 241 males and 1,095 females were murdered by an intimate partner (U.S. Department of Justice, FBI, 2011).

Physical violence causes debilitating physical injuries and severe and lasting psychological damage to victims, as well as to children who routinely see or hear one parent physically attacking the other.

In periods leading up to acute battery, there can be a series of less traumatic physical mistreatment resulting in relatively minor injuries. These abuses are often used to intimidate or retaliate against a victim for violating a rule imposed by the abuser, such as restricting use of money or forbidding contact with family or friends. Though perhaps not life-threatening, these other forms of physical abuse are very serious. They include shoving, biting, grabbing, pulling hair, slapping, as well as damaging property and even hurting the victim's pets.

Physical abuse also includes using various means to restrain the victim, or, what is called "false imprisonment." Second Chance clients have been locked in the house and locked in closets. In one case, the windows were nailed shut to keep the victim from leaving. One woman was chained to a fixture in the house for days. Although physical restraint is not unusual, it is not typically a part of what I call domestic captivity, which takes place with and without physical means of false imprisonment.

Physical violence is not the result of a normal disagreement or irresolvable conflict between intimate partners. Conflict may trigger, or serve as a pretense for, an attack. But conflict simply cannot explain the malady we call domestic violence. In the end, domestic violence is not about conflict. It is about control. This is why conflict resolution techniques, though effective in other contexts, do not stop domestic violence. Physical abuse is best understood as one aspect of the systematic mistreatment, whereby a domestic partner gains control over and imposes captivity on the other.

Verbal Abuse

A defining characteristic of verbal abuse is the use of words to undermine the victim's value and identity. Verbal abuse is not simply unkind speech one might hear in the heat of an argument, words one might use in anger and later regret. Verbal abuse entails the psychological beating down of a person.

Verbal abuse includes menacing speech. A verbally abusive person often threatens physical violence against the victim, and against her children, other relations, pets, cherished property. Another common abuse is the abuser's threat to harm or kill himself.

Verbal abuse typically involves cruel and vulgar terms to put down the woman's intelligence and appearance. Many victims are repeatedly told that no one else would "put up with" them, and that they could not survive without the abuser. As we saw in Diane's story, abusers describe in lurid detail the harm they intend to do to the victims. Verbal put-downs and threatening behaviors tend to grow in intensity and frequency over time.

In addition to its direct hurtfulness and coercion, verbal abuse is also used in more subtle psychological manipulation. For example, in intimate relationships that are or will become violent, the use of flattering or complimentary words as a means of manipulation and control could be considered verbal abuse, though I don't think I've heard it expressly labeled as such. It is a kind of abuse by deception that tends to occur when the abuser has reason to think the victim is entertaining ideas of separation, such as in the time following an acute attack. A woman, who had been demeaned with the cruelest names imaginable, then hears that she is the most beautiful woman to walk the earth, and is the object of the batterer's undying devotion. He may confess the error of his ways and promise to change. In reality, the abuser remains an abuser, as long as the relationship continues, even as he manipulates her with speech of this nature.

The verbal abuse of seduction figures prominently in the courtship stage of relationships that later turn violent. Vulnerabilities are exploited, in the incremental entrapment before more noticeable signs of abuse ever appear.

Psychological Abuse

It's hard to think of any abuse—whether physical, verbal, or economic, that is not also psychological abuse. Although it is often useful to think of the discrete psychological components of various types of abuse, for purposes of this book, I tend to consider psychological harm as a part of the damage done by every form of abuse.

Economic Abuse

While there are many abuses that contribute to domestic captivity, there is none more potent than economic abuse. In Diane's story, we see the power of economic abuse when perpetrated by an affluent abuser. But the disempowering impact of economic abuse is no less effective in mid-or low-income households.

CHAPTER 9

Forms of Abuse Continued: Economic Abuse

Second Chance's success in liberating victims of domestic violence is largely due to measures that counter economic abuse with economic empowerment.

While physical battering, verbal and psychological abuse are well known aspects of domestic violence, there is far less awareness of abuses that relate to deprivation of material well-being. Economic abuse is just not something that springs to mind at the mention of domestic violence. This not to say anyone is surprised to learn that a violently abusive person also oppresses the victim financially. But financial maltreatment has not traditionally been examined as a separate form of abusive behavior, or for its role in the captivity of domestic violence victims that allows physical violence to continue.

The CDC report released in December 2011 defines domestic violence as "physical, sexual, or psychological harm by a current or former partner or spouse."[27] Although 'psychological harm" is broad enough to encompass many types of abuse, including economic abuse, it is notable that the government's official definition does not examine economic abuse as a discrete form of abuse. There are a number of reasons to do so.

Economic abuse is nearly always present when there is physical violence in an intimate relationship. It consists of acts and omissions distinct from other kinds of abuse. Economic abuse is crucial to the abuser's gaining control over the victim and preventing her from ending the violent relationship. Recognizing economic abuse as a distinct form was essential to me in developing a systematic approach to facilitating lifelong freedom.

Depriving the victim of control over her own economic well-being is a despotic and confining element of domestic violence. It imposes both physical and psychological barriers to escaping the violence.

When I founded Second Chance, scholars and other experts were aware that economic dependence played a significant role in domestic violence. However, economic abuse was not considered a distinct form of abuse or a particular aspect of domestic violence, let alone an essential element. With Second Chance's hundreds of success stories, and the "Second Chance Provision" recently added to the VAWA, economic abuse should no longer be overlooked as a distinct element of domestic violence.

The 2008 Adams study stands out as one of the very few studies to recognize "economic abuse" as a separate form of abuse, and a significant element of control in violent intimate partnerships. Second Chance has administered surveys to hundreds of our clients over the course of many years. Our data demonstrate, in the nature and impact of economically abusive behavior, a disturbing consistency.

Among the survey questions we asked of our clients is the following: "Did the abuser use financial power as a means of control?" For "yes" answers, a space is provided to write an explanation. Printed below are representative responses of 22 client-survivors, in their own words:

1. He used finances to control me. Made it difficult to leave. I was afraid of being alone . . . not thinking I could support myself.

2. He took all my money and had control of everything in my life.
3. "You have no say-so," he used to say. Since he became the only [source of] income he thought he had the only say-so.
4. He was very controlling with everything in order to keep me in "check."
5. He had 100% control of me.
6. It was always a problem when it was about financials.
7. I could not talk about money needed without getting beaten down.
8. I depended on my husband.
9. I was unable to do anything; he would pay for everything. No access to income.
10. He became massively controlling, even with my money.
11. He would use financial power as a means of control.
12. My ex was my main provider so he used to abuse that power against me.
13. He became sick and controlling, even with my money.
14. He wouldn't give me money whenever we fought.
15. He had all the power over the relationship.
16. One of his tactics of manipulation was withholding money ... [for necessary things].
17. He was the only one working so he had financial control.
18. I became a homemaker who depended 100% on her husband.
19. Whatever I needed had to be justified and explained.
20. Mental abuse on what I would buy controlling and counting what money I had.
21. I had to shop together with him.
22. He controlled the money. If I said save some for a rainy day he would get angry or violent.

These descriptions of economic abuse, representative of the experiences of countless other survivors, show quite clearly the relationship between economic abuse and domestic captivity. The connection is especially clear in responses like the following from another Second Chance client:

> My mate didn't want me to leave the house without him to go shopping.... He would not give me money to go anywhere because he wanted me in the house.

Our clients' responses to the survey support two aspects of economic abuse that inform the Second Chance approach. The same two aspects are also documented in the Adams study: First, a "direct consequence of economic abuse . . . is that the survivor becomes economically dependent on the abuser";[28] and second, "economic dependence [is] a critical obstacle for many women who are attempting to leave abusive partners."[29]

The Adams study breaks down economic abuse into three subcategories. In particular, according to the article, economic abuse occurs when the perpetrator interferes with a victim's ability to (1) acquire, (2) use, or (3) maintain economic resources.[30]

Acquisition of resources

"One significant way that abusive men interfere with a woman's ability to acquire resources is by preventing her from obtaining and maintaining employment. . . . Abusive men often forbid, discourage, and actively prevent their partners from working outside the home."[31]

Specific tactics used to block the victims from acquiring resources include: making her too embarrassed to appear in public by inflicting unsightly injuries, or cutting off the victim's hair; inflicting injuries that make mobility difficult; turning off alarm clocks to prevent the victim from getting to work on time; neglecting care of small children; refusing to provide for professional childcare; stealing the victim's car keys or money (or both); sabotaging car used to drive to work; not allowing her to have her own car; physically restraining the victim; withholding needed medication; preventing sleep; hiding her clothes; harassing her at work by showing up, or calling her multiple times throughout the day; harassing the victim's co-workers; interfering with efforts at self-improvement, for example, interfering with ability to further education.[32]

The foregoing tactics, most of which are listed in the Adams study, match the experiences of Second Chance clients. Some illustrative examples from our internal surveys:

- He threatened [to tell] the owners of the company to terminate me, when I didn't allow him to do whatever he wanted.
- I wasn't allowed to work, leave from home without his permission.
- The reason for leaving [former employer is that] I was too embarrassed to go [to work] with a black eye.
- He cut up all my clothes, stole $1600 for me to get my own place, stole purse with ID's.

Notice that many of these tactics interfering with the acquisition of resources not only stop financial independence but also remove freedoms of mobility and association. As such, it is an abuse of isolation, and contributes to psychological depression, and the strength of domestic captivity.

Another frequently used tactic to prevent victims from earning an income is to block them from pursuing higher education or vocational training. One of our clients acquiesced to her violent husband's demand that she drop out of medical school. Another, who had a graduate degree that predated the abusive relationship, wrote simply, "I was not allowed to work." Still another explained, "I wanted to go to school [and] needed help with the child." In her case, the battering spouse used outlandish behavior to sabotage the woman's ability to hire a babysitter.

I've had a number of clients who have been permitted to work only for their abusive husband's business. This allows him to control her income—if any—and also leaves her with only one reference to cite for any future employment—the abuser. The abuser deters her from looking for a job and, in the event she does try, hinders her chances of being hired. One client earned her DDS degree to pursue her dream of becoming a dentist. But her husband would not permit her to sit for the board exam to be licensed, and insisted that she work only for him. Together with the other abuse of physical and psychological brutality, he deprived her of power to leave. In spite of her advanced degree and medical training, her will to pursue her dreams was forced into dormancy.

Second Chance clients also recount instances of the abuser having stolen their car keys; and stopping them from buying clothes needed for work or job interviews. Physical restraint, combined with other tactics, is not unusual. One client recalled, "he would lock me in the house, [t]ake the house keys, make sure there wasn't any money available."

Jane was a Second Chance client who, before her relationship with the abuser, had been a successful businesswoman. Her abusive partner, having gained increasing levels of control over her life, persuaded her to give up her job. She later decided to re-enter the work force. But after she'd been on her new job for a few days, he managed to get her fired. He did so by showing up at her new office, shouting wildly, and menacing Jane and her co-workers with vile curses and threatening movements. There at the office he threatened to beat her and set her on fire. Jane and her co-workers were naturally traumatized. Though she obtained a civil protection order, her new manager was so badly shaken by the incident that he refused to continue her employment.

Another woman who came to Second Chance had been fired when her abuser, who was in jail at the time, sent a gang of friends to harass her at work. With some frequency our clients have been blocked by their abusers from obtaining the legal immigration status needed to work in the United States.

A client told us she did not find a job because she was "too depressed to look for work." This is a simple statement representative of a commonly occurring problem for victims of domestic violence. Sustained mistreatment by a domestic partner induces a debilitating depression that prevents the victim from even trying to find a job. Behavior attacking the victim's self-worth, interfering with her appreciation of her own individual gifts, has the effect of undermining hope of a better life. Inducing depression of this sort, abusers may powerfully interfere with a victim's ability to acquire resources. Depression, more generally, is a major contributing factor to the paralysis that precludes escape from the abusive relationship.

Abuse that induces depression is again parallel to tactics of autocratic regimes that deliberately dehumanize people, leaving them so dejected and despondent as to force into dormancy the natural will to pursue individual dreams and happiness.

Ability to Use Resources

With respect to hindering the victims' ability to use resources, Adams' study documents abuses that again match the histories of many Second Chance clients: denying all access to money for necessities such as food; allocating a certain (often inadequate) amount to be spent on necessities and nothing more; requiring the victim to ask for money; hiding money; preventing victim from having access to joint bank accounts; lying about shared assets; generally withholding information about finances; and controlling and prohibiting transportation by taking car keys, disabling the car, and so forth.[33]

A Second Chance client reported that her partner, a medical doctor, gave her $10.00 a day for food for herself and her 18 year old son. Other than that, she said, "I had no access to money." The following additional examples taken from the Second Chance surveys amount to a tragic chorus of heartless abuse, and part of the system of domestic tyranny and captivity:

- He did not give me money, only what was needed.
- He would get aggressive whenever I would ask for money for basic needs of the baby.
- He would not help out with the baby expenses.
- He would give money for baby expenses. He would not contribute towards my personal expenses, such [as] clothing....
- I was not allowed to pay bills nor access to money.
- If I asked for money I would get beat up.
- He would choose even my clothing. I can't freely use the money he gives for expenses.
- My husband doesn't give me money for personal necessities. Whenever I ask there's a fight.
- I worked for a business he owned and he'd sometimes hold my paycheck.
- I couldn't buy my own clothes or food, etc.
- I was not allowed to spend my money as I . . . desired and had to account for every dollar and could not use discretionary income on myself without clearing it with him first.
- He wouldn't give me money to go to work. He made sure that I didn't have access to any of the credit cards or any bank card.
- When I was not working he refused to buy anything with his earnings which often led to arguments.
- He would claim [necessary things were] a waste of money. [Since I was] not working . . . I [could not] join in decision-making.
- He paid the rent and gave me nothing else. I applied for food stamps. And that's how I could buy food. . . . He would only give me money for the necessities.
- He only gave me from $16.00 - $20.00 cash a month. I was forbidden from opening a bank account or sharing or using his credit or debit cards. No clothing. No toiletries. Made me ask for money. I didn't know where to go because he controlled me.

The abusive spouse of one of my clients, used violence and other coercion to forbid her from earning an income, then stopped paying power bills. During a winter that was exceptionally cold, in which there were several large snow storms, he moved by himself to a separate dwelling, abandoning her and their small children to live without heat in the frigid home through the entire winter. This kind of tactic is not unusual. Studies in 1993 and 2003, among others, included reports of abused partners who have had their heat, electricity, and phone turned off.[34]

The violent partners of Second Chance clients have taken out credit card accounts in the victim's name only. It may seem hard to believe that a domestic abuser would purposefully destroy the victim's credit rating. In fact, the tactic is very frequently reported by our clients:

- He grew angry when I did not allow him to use my ATM card, would take it and spend large amounts of money, affecting my credit.
- He would take my credit cards and bank cards and spend large amounts of money that I didn't have in the bank and then bring the cards back to me for me to pay the debt on.

Because they affect one's mobility and ability to acquire resources, poor credit ratings can seriously restrict individual freedom. Also, there's a growing trend of employers checking prospective employee's credit rating. So, destroying the credit of the victim is another factor keeping victims from finding employment and becoming economically self-sufficient.

By maxing out the victim's credit cards, and not making payments on them, the abuser perpetrates two forms of economic abuse. He interferes with her acquisition of resources by wrecking her credit rating; and at the same time he exploits and depletes the credit resources she has.

Exploiting and Depleting Resources

The exploitation and depletion of resources is another form of abuse, or subcategory of hindering ability to use resources.[35] The tactic diminishes the victim's power to provide for herself and her children. It precludes accumulation of assets that might provide financial security or an ability to live independently of the abuser. The effect, again is to disempower the victim and foster a sense of dependence on the abuser.[36]

Second Chance clients tell of many instances of depletion of resources, by stealing money directly, by creating costs, and generating debt. The accounts of these survivors are not isolated incidents but a common abuse that occurs in intimate partner relationships. This is borne out by a study summarized in the Adams article:

> . . . [A study in 2003] reported the frequency of stealing among a sample of 485 women who sought services from a domestic abuse advocacy program. It was determined that 38% of the women reported that their partners stole money from them. According to anecdotal reports from other victim advocates, abusive men steal money from their partners through a variety of means. An abusive man may take money from his partner's purse or wallet, steal her checkbook or ATM card and use it without permission, gamble with her money or shared money, or demand that her money be put into a joint bank account so that he can spend it freely.[37]

Abusive men also cause damage to apartments, houses, and cars.[38] As we've seen, they cut off power and other utilities. These and other tactics deplete women's economic resources not only by depriving them of property they once had, but also by costs incurred to reinstate utilities and other services, replace items, and repair the damage.

The following tactics to deplete the victim's resources were reported by our clients in the Second Chance surveys:

- If I did not give him the money he would hit me.
- He said he didn't have money. I would pay majority of the bills.
- Whenever I bring my money or check home I was forced to give it to him and he will spend the money on alcohol and mostly on him self.
- He wanted her to pay rent and take care of other things and continue to harass her.
- Every time I got paid or received any money it was given to him. He had no job but being a Muslim man he still was considered head of the house or "the banker."
- He would spend [the money] or say I don't have any left. He also would steal my money that I did have."
- [He] was very controlling with our finances; often spent more than he made and ultimately borrowed money to keep living.

Stealing from the victim is often reported in cases where the batterer is addicted to alcohol or drugs. This also is reflected in our clients' survey responses:

- He was an addict. He *would steal money from me.*
- He was an alcoholic and he got drunk and hit me and would *force me to give him money.*
- Would steal money saying he's holding it or he would use it to buy drugs.
- He would take my money and spend it on drugs.

CHAPTER 10

Domestic Disempowerment

Whether the dominion is a public state, or a private household, the cumulative impact of the three broad categories of abuse is disempowerment. Put another way, the tyranny of abuses deprives the victim of freedom, leaving her in a state of paralysis and captivity.

The types of power or freedom taken through physical, verbal and economic abuse generally fit into the categories that follow.

Freedom of Expression

A defining characteristic of totalitarianism is the prohibition of free expression. Typically under such systems, speech critical of the government is expressly forbidden by law.

Similarly, victims of domestic violence and human trafficking are discouraged and, in many cases, effectively prohibited from expressing themselves. We saw an appalling example of this in Diane's story. Tyrants use restriction of speech to intimidate and control victims while inhibiting outside knowledge of the abuse. Thus, in domestic tyranny, free speech is curtailed both inside and outside the home.

Freedom of Association

Closely related to curtailment of free expression are restrictions on associations. In a tyrannical regime, citizens are prohibited from associating with certain individuals and entities, especially associations formed out of disaffection with ruling authority. One must not associate with anyone who could be considered seditious, disloyal, or even critical. Laws against free association are part of the broader strategy of control by isolation. The sovereign knows there is power in numbers. By separating people from each other, he disempowers his subjects, and so bolsters his own authority and control.

A domestic tyrant imposes analogous restrictions on associations, usually with scope and severity that increases over time. Associations perceived as a threat to the abuser's control are naturally subject to the most intense control. Family, close friends, clergy, counselors, social service agencies, support groups, and the like, are prime targets for exclusion. To the extent associations are tolerated, the terms and circumstances of interaction may fall subject to increasing control.

To remove the freedom of association is by definition to impose isolation. Isolation is the "iron curtain" of domestic tyranny. It is essential to domestic captivity. It allows the perpetrator to commit crimes against the victim in secret, keeping outsiders from seeing in, and victims from reaching out. It thus magnifies the abuser's power to inflict further abuse of every type. The freedom to associate may be removed, and isolation imposed, by physical, verbal, or economic abuses, or any combination of these. Isolation is imposed verbally, for example, by threatening repercussions for any attempt to tell others about the mistreatment, or to seek support outside the relationship.

A common line is that no one would believe her story, especially after she remained with him for so long. The abuser may tell the victim that if she communicates with her family or friends, he will punish her physically, or by withholding money or other resources. He may threaten her with bodily injury if she sees a counselor or attends a support group. Another method used to prevent association is the type of physical restraint previously discussed. We frequently hear that attempts to use social networking media, and electronic communication with potential sources of help is forbidden and punished. Women have been badly beaten when caught visiting an internet site offering support for battered women. Aware of the danger, websites of support organizations have begun to include a button for a quick "disguised" exit from the site. Clicking on the button instantly closes all web pages associated with the site while simultaneously opening an innocuous-looking decoy page, and every trace of the support site is automatically deleted from the "history" of the browser. Features such as this speak volumes about the reality and intensity of isolation and captivity.

For many victims, anxiety about being blamed for problems in the marriage and the resulting shame contribute to the isolation.

Second Chance clients have reported being forbidden to have any friends outside his own social circle. This level of control over associations reveals the extent of repression of basic freedom that takes place within a domestic tyranny.

Isolation causes depression, is generally demoralizing, and can be psychologically harmful. In this way too, the abuse of isolation enhances the abuser's control over the victim and enforces the state of captivity.

As shown in Part Two, the disempowering effects of isolation are counteracted by Second Chance's network of healthy relationships.

Freedom of Belief, Freedom of Conscience

Verbal abuse combines with extreme physical and economic maltreatment to control the victim's thoughts and beliefs. We saw this in Diane's transformed opinions about herself and her former beliefs.

It is common in violent intimate partnerships for physical and verbal abuse combined with economic deprivation to convey the ever-present propaganda: the victim is worthless, she has no identity, and no ability to survive without the abuser. Physical beating combined with verbal threats and removal of access to money and other resources intimidate, frighten, and otherwise coerce the victim. The victim will not only do what the abuser commands, but also change her beliefs to conform to the abuser's. The tyranny of this kind of mind control is a powerful bar to her escape.

Abusive speech repeats and reinforces negative messages that are also conveyed by physical, economic and other mistreatment. Over a period of many years, the victim will hear on a daily basis messages like the following: you are worthless"; "no one but [the abuser] would tolerate you"; "you would not survive without me." The same lies are communicated with fists and other physical abuse, as well as by withholding economic necessities.

A well-known aspect of totalitarian states is the need to control the people's thoughts. A dictator may use propaganda, coercion by physical force, threats, and deprivation to indoctrinate the multitude with ways of thinking that support his power and control. The same tactics are used to expunge from public and private belief all systems of thought that are potentially incompatible with his absolute authority.

In many cases, totalitarian states have been actively involved in controlling religious beliefs as well. In ancient Rome, pagan beliefs and rituals were part of everyday life, and a common article of faith was the belief that the emperor was a god. The deified Caesar was to be revered, worshipped, and feared above all others. On his providence and forbearance the people depended. Roman subjects were permitted to worship certain other gods; however, they must not prefer any before Caesar. To eradicate the promotion of a preeminent God some Roman emperors persecuted followers of Jesus, with infamous cruelty such as burning them at the stake, or throwing them to the lions.

From medieval times through the 19th century, the absolute power of English monarchs was justified by the "divine right" doctrine of kingship. To rebel against the king, or to question his authority, was to rebel against God himself.

Under these English and Roman autocracies, and many others through the ages, people were forbidden to believe as they wished. Freedom of conscience, freedom of religion, posed a direct threat to the exclusive authority and control of the ruling class. Subjects were made to live in fear and awe of the all-powerful king. By making them dependent on his providence and protection, a sovereign could hope to arouse natural gratitude and loyalty. Should contrary thoughts and feelings intrude on a subject's loyalty to the monarch, guilt and fear could also be powerful forces to help keep their minds and hearts in check.

The latter state of mind bears a strong resemblance to the psychological impact of tyranny on victims of domestic violence. At some point in the abusive relationship, many are effectively forbidden to practice their religious faith or tradition, and kept through various means from spiritual activity in general. Curtailment of religious practice and belief is accompanied by efforts to replace existing beliefs with a different sort of religion.

If not overtly claiming to be a demigod like the Roman emperors, domestic abusers to varying degrees lay claim to the equivalent of a "divine right" to rule over their intimate partners. The victims must accept his authority as infallible. Thoughts and actions contrary to his authority are offenses against the order of the universe. Under domestic tyranny, as under a state tyranny, control over the victims' thoughts is a significant aspect of the disempowerment that holds them in captivity.

Economic Freedom

Not surprisingly, ideologies favored by totalitarian regimes tend to promote a culture of dependence on the sovereign. An autocrat portrays himself as necessary to the security of the people and their children against all dangers, and for the basic provisions needed for life: food, clothing and shelter. The people must be made to realize they are incapable of surviving without the providence and protection of the ruler.

Examples in history abound of systematic economic repression being used by despotic rulers to exercise control over a populace. Creating dependence on the state for basic necessities and security works

But the will to pursue her dream was forced into dormancy by domestic tyranny. Even as totalitarian regimes use various types of abuse to prevent their people from using their natural talents to gain wealth and power, the private despot of this woman's life had deprived her of the power to use hers.

There is no more prominent characteristic of the imbalance of power in domestic violence than the abuser's removal of economic freedom. The loss of this freedom is a major aspect of her inability to escape. We see the deprivation in nearly every Second Chance client, even in those who do not recognize it themselves. With the multiplicity of other repressions, the removal of financial freedom contributes to physical and emotional dependence on the abuser, analogous to the constraints imposed by state tyrants. Because economic freedom is a major element in overcoming the paralysis, financial empowerment is at the center of Second Chance's antidote.

CHAPTER 11

Processes of Disempowerment

Whether by an intuitive, unconscious process, or a deliberate strategy, the process of disempowerment occurs incrementally and cumulatively. It tends to involve unpredictable, seemingly arbitrary swings between extremes in behavior and treatment.

Pre-captivity: Entrapment Phase

How did a domestic violence victim end up in a violent relationship? Consenting adults are free to decide whether to marry or enter an intimate partnership. No one forces them into it by physical capture. In the many years I have been serving victims of domestic violence, I have yet to find one who entered into an intimate relationship knowing or believing the man would turn out to be abusive. Despite the recent popularity of certain fiction glamorizing relationships involving domination and submission, a victim of domestic violence has not entered the abusive relationship voluntarily. It is not a consensual relationship and probably it never was. How is this possible?

I have a friend who is a lawyer who told me about a legal maxim, "fraud vitiates consent." Suppose a man promises to give you a diamond if you run a marathon. Normally, you would not run a marathon, but after seeing the diamond in his hand, you agree to do it. So you run the marathon and the person gives you the jewel. But later you find out the thing you got was actually cubic zirconia, worth a fraction of the value of a diamond that size. Did you run the marathon voluntarily? No! You promised to run in exchange for a certain thing, and you would not have run without the promise of that thing; you never promised to run for the thing you actually got. Fraud canceled your consent.

This is what happens in the initial stages of many intimate relationships that later become violent. The future abuser induces the victim to enter the relationship by deception. He presents himself as a loving person, respectful of her autonomy. She enters the relationship thinking he is a certain man; but he was another sort of person altogether. Had she known his actual violent and abusive character, she would not have agreed to the relationship. Because the relationship was formed in reliance on false pretenses, it is not a voluntary or consensual relationship. Fraud vitiates consent.

I am not saying victims of abuse are always without emotional issues, or that they always make perfect decisions. I am saying that whatever flaws a person may have, such imperfections do not explain why a woman finds herself subject to the brutality of a violent intimate partner. In many cases, it is the fraudulent misrepresentations of the abuser.

A persistent fiction about victims of domestic violence is that they are secretly or unconsciously drawn to abusive personalities. Some try to support the idea by pointing to women who move from one abusive relationship to another. From such a pattern, a conclusion is drawn that the victim is secretly seeking an abusive relationship.

There is a much more plausible explanation and one consistent with my experience. The abusive personality is the one who is drawn to people who are most vulnerable to the deception and control. He may reject or be rejected by many women who prove not to have the right traits, before he finds someone whom he can control. Women who become victims may have a trusting nature, a lack of cynicism, or a belief that love is possible by making oneself vulnerable.

We asked one of our clients at Second Chance how she ended up marrying a man who had subjected her to terrible violence. She said,

> [E]specially with someone that you love and trust and your guard is down, you don't have any reason to think that this person is going to do anything to hurt you—I mean love doesn't hurt—so you trust them you're open, you're vulnerable and they know you're vulnerable . . . and then what they do is they use that against you . . . .

This attitude hardly supports the idea that a woman who becomes a victim of domestic violence was looking for an abusive man to marry. The abuser was able to entrap her because she understood trust and vulnerability to be the price of genuine love in intimate relationships.

Perpetrators of abuse may also seek out women who are insecure, or do not have high self-confidence to begin with. One survivor said, "My [initial] attraction to him, which never occurred to me at the time, came from a basic need for security and meaning." Another one of our clients shared an insight she had learned in counseling: the abandonment by her father at an early age left her trying always to please people in relationships so that they would not reenact the abandonment by her father.

The need for security and a meaningful relationship is a far cry from a secret desire to be abused. There are abusers who take advantage of these needs, perhaps instinctively, and twist them into dependence of the victim on himself. In the beginning stages of captivity in what I sometimes call the "entrapment" stage, it is basic human needs like these, combined with a willingness to be vulnerable, that makes a person susceptible to the fraud that cancels consent.

Whatever the reason, the fact that one enters a relationship that turns violent is no reason to blame the victim, or think that she voluntarily entered an abusive relationship.

The Abuse is Incremental and Intermittent

In 1788, James Madison noted "there are more instances of the abridgement of the freedom of the people by gradual and silent encroachments of those in power, than by violent and sudden usurpations." The reason for an incremental approach to taking power is simple enough. A sudden dramatic change would be more likely to trigger armed resistance, or flight. To avoid jarring the target of a conquest into evasive action before control is solidified, the invading power moves in barely perceptible increments. By tightening the grip of oppression by degrees, the loss of freedom is not perceived until after the balance of power has already shifted and the subject is no longer able to escape.

A "sudden usurpation" in the context of domestic relations is very unlikely. Domestic abusers encroach upon the victim's freedoms by degrees, and gradually take control of her physical person, thoughts and emotions, over a period of months or years.

In addition to growing intensity, another variable in the process of disempowering and paralyzing the victim is the frequency of abuse. Because the first instances may be infrequent, they are easier to dismiss as aberrations or explained away as normal conflict, or otherwise justified by circumstances.

At first the abuse may be almost imperceptible, so small and trivial that any objection can be characterized as unreasonable. With greater degrees of emotional and physical attachment, when the victim has more at stake, the level and frequency of abuse gets more frequent and more serious. Moving in together obviously signals a major change in the level of commitment. And deepening commitment (combined with heightened vulnerability) is another reason why abuse frequently becomes markedly more severe when the woman becomes pregnant.

With each occurrence of verbal, physical, economic, and other abuse, the victim's freedoms are gradually taken away, and her power grows smaller by degrees. The incremental and intermittent nature of this weaving latticework helps explain how a victim comes to be trapped in domestic captivity.

The denial that her partner could be abusing her may continue even as he threatens serious harm, pushes her, or destroys or threatens to destroy her property. Even with the onset of punching, kicking or other battery, the victim often denies that she is a battered woman. Part of this is explained by what Walker refers to as the loving contrition, or remorse phase of the cycle of violence. The interval between acute battery and the tension building phases is characterized by tender contrition and romantic gestures, reminiscent of the courting period. So, even as the abuse gets more serious, the victim may dismiss the abuse as uncharacteristic, an aberration, a "one-off" incident.

Little by little, without her noticing, avenues of escape are cut off—physically, psychologically, economically. At a certain point, so many of her former freedoms have been taken that the victim finds herself in captivity. She finds herself isolated and trapped. "All power is on the side of the oppressor and there is none to comfort" her.

Upon a particularly severe episode of abuse, she may flee. But even after leaving the house, and moving into the safety of a battered woman's shelter, the vortex of domestic partner abuse continues to exert power over her; it draws her back into his arms, even though he has already committed violent crimes against her.

The Abuse is Unpredictable

Although there is a "cycle of violence," the cycle is not necessarily predictable. In fact, an abuser's behavior may be extremely erratic. One moment the woman is told she is worthless and ugly; a short time later, he says her beauty is beyond compare, and she is his only reason to live. In the morning, he may revere her as a saint and come home in the evening to revile her as a demon. She has no way to predict at any given moment whether she will be put on a pedestal or thrown down the stairs.

Unpredictability is itself a kind of abuse, and disempowering in a number of ways. Flattering compliments temporarily allay doubts about the relationship, rekindle hopes that things might be getting better. Then thoughts she was having about leaving him seem to be overreactions. From vicious cruelty to flattering, romantic words, or expressions of remorse: such dramatic changes are disarming, and can leave the victim off-balance.

On the swing of the pendulum to the positive side, the abuser exploits her hope that he'll change, that there's no need to leave after all. The pendulum swings back and her hopes are dashed. She is further demoralized and destabilized, maybe ashamed. The vacillations naturally cause greater anxiety and depression.

The pendulum is not a perfect comparison because the swings of a pendulum are predictable. The abuser's behavior can flip from day to night in a heartbeat, with no intervening dusk or dawn to signal a change. What's worse, there may be no connection between what the victim says or does and the sudden shift of behavior. If the abuser gives a reason, the connection tends to be, from an objective viewpoint, irrational.

One of our clients was beaten by her abuser and had to be rushed to the hospital with serious injuries. That night, he showed up at the hospital room. As she lay there in crippling pain, he told her he "didn't mean it," promised never to hurt her again, told her how beautiful she was, that he loved and adored her and would do anything for her. A few days later he broke mirrors and ripped up the upholstery in their bedroom. This succession of changes, from criminal battery, to tender words, to violent destruction of property, had no connection to anything she had said or done.

Diane described the unpredictable atmosphere with her abusive husband as "walking on eggshells." A harmless comment on a trivial matter could trigger a vicious attack, catching her totally by surprise. Even agreeing with him, she said, could be perilous because he would accuse her of "just trying to appease him." Remaining silent might also get her in trouble if he thought she was ignoring him. On more than one occasion he had flown into a rage because she did not say anything.

Even though unpredictability and dramatic shifts seem irrational, there may be a method to the madness. In addition to the direct impact already mentioned, there is a more subtle way in which erratic behavior disempowers the victim. If she could stop the abuse by conforming to his expectations, she would maintain at least some measure of control. She would be able modify her behavior to please him and avoid repercussions.

Arbitrary, unpredictable behavior deprives her of any measure of control, and enhances his power over her. She might do everything in perfect conformity with his demands and still be subject to intense hostility; or she might fret all day about his reaction to some big mistake, only to find him docile and affectionate in response. In sum, she has no power to influence whether he will treat her as a princess or a piece of trash.

There is a form of unpredictability that occurs in the context of economic abuse. Frequently, abusers vacillate between provision and deprivation. The provision of money or necessary material things may be made conditional on the victim's compliance; or withheld arbitrarily. The victim is made to feel she and her children are not only at the mercy of the one who has assumed control over the finances, but that there is no way to predict or have any influence over whether he will provide for the family's material needs.

Arbitrary shifts in economic behavior take oppression to a more painful level. If the victim were able to obtain needed things by complying with a set of rules, she would at least have some control over whether she and her children would have clothes to wear or food to eat. By when there is no rhyme or reason to availability of resources, and when even obeying strict and unjust rules are no guaranty of access, a more intense level of anxiety and desperation befall her. With cruel unpredictability, a small remnant of control over her circumstances is yanked away. In the area of material needs for herself and her children, nothing is left but instability.

The arbitrary action and inaction also serves to intensify the victim's sense of dependency and fear of destitution. It may make her more susceptible to manipulation, more inclined to believe lies about her being utterly unable to live without his provision.

The Abuse is Cumulative

Not one form of abuse, but overlapping various forms work together to establish tyrannical control over the victim. Even the most iron-fisted government does not prevent mass emigration of a people solely by force and threat of force. Physically restraining the movement of an entire population would entail an allocation of resources that would be undesirable and, in fact, unnecessary to accomplish containment. Also, contemporary dictators are scrutinized by other nations and may be subject to sanctions for human rights violations, making it necessary to create at least the appearance of voluntary citizenship. Creating such an appearance reduces the ability to rely on brute force alone to keep citizens from leaving. So, a combination of tactics are used to repress and immobilize the population, and to inculcate a sense of dependency on the ruler.

An analogous abuse of power occurs in domestic tyranny. Overlapping and intermittent combinations of abusive behaviors work together to deprive the victim of the power to leave the relationship—and even the power to think about living independently as a realistic option. It is the cumulative impact of several kinds of dehumanizing mistreatment, physical and non-physical, that allows an abuser to assert control over the victim, and eventually deprive her of power and freedom to separate from him.

We've seen illustrations of the devastation of complex abuses in the narratives and in quotes from survey responses. Another one of our clients described how she endured economic abuses together with physical and verbal battering. She said, "when given financial support,

I was often told [by abuser] that no one else would ever have me, that I was not employable." As may be inferred from the statement, the abuser controlled her access to and use of financial resources. Behind the statement, "when given financial support" was the reality that he routinely did not give it. Significantly, she says the financial "support" was "often" accompanied with a verbal assault, telling the victim, in essence, that she was worthless and "not employable."

Abusers frequently tell their victims that they are not employable, while at the same time creating financial dependency. Communicating fictitious worthlessness is done verbally, as in the statement above, and by physical beatings and threats. Financial dependence, combined with verbal and physical abuse when repeated over a course of years, takes away the victim's power to terminate the relationship.

CHAPTER 12

Human Trafficking

We tend to think of slavery as a thing of the past. But in our contemporary world, in the midst of societies that greatly value freedom, there's an epidemic of slavery. It goes by the name of "human trafficking."

The core problem of human trafficking, like that of intimate partner violence, is domestic captivity, imposed by means of a secret tyranny over the victim. Because the fundamental cause of the victim's predicament is the same, the same solution is effective. The Second Chance system has proven effective in emancipating those enslaved through trafficking.

Human trafficking is defined by U.S. and international authorities as criminal activity used to hold a person in involuntary service. The Victims of Trafficking and Violence Protection Act (TVPA) divides human trafficking into two general categories: sex trafficking and forced labor trafficking.

The U.S. State Department defines an adult victim of sex trafficking as a person who is "coerced, forced, or deceived into prostitution, or maintained in prostitution through coercion."[39] The United Nations' defines the phenomenon as follows: "The recruitment, transportation, transfer, harbouring or receipt of persons, by means of threat or use of force or other forms of coercion, of abduction, of fraud, of deception, of the abuse of power or of a position of vulnerability or the giving or receiving of payments or benefits to achieve the consent of a person having control over another person, for the purpose of exploitation."[40] As used by the UN here, "exploitation" includes "the prostitution of others or other forms of sexual exploitation, forced labor or services, slavery or practices similar to slavery, servitude or the removal of organs."

Worldwide, approximately 12.3 million adults and children presently live under the enslavement of human trafficking. It is estimated that sex trafficking accounts for 80% and labor trafficking 18% of victims. Fifty-six percent of all forced labor victims are women and girls. About 800,000 - 900,000 victims are trafficked annually across international borders worldwide. Of these, about 18,000-20,000 are brought into United States. They are trafficked from, among other places, Africa, Asia, India, Latin America, Eastern Europe, Russia and Canada. More than half of them are minor children.

A limitless variety of exploitative circumstances ensnare victims in slavery. Trafficking victims are trapped by a series of fraudulent misrepresentations, by coercion, threats, physical battery, and false imprisonment. They may be disorientated by numerous relocations, enduring barbaric conditions. Before realizing how it has happened, they find themselves in unfamiliar geographical regions and cultures, and practically unbreakable dependency on their captors.

The slavery goes largely unnoticed by the surrounding community. A host of factors account for the invisibility. A recurring factor is that many victims do not speak the language of the country in which they are sold. They are therefore unable to communicate effectively with service providers, police, and others in a position to help. The language barrier contributes to isolation and magnifies the power of those who control them. Many are coerced into silence also by the captors' warnings that reporting the situation would result in the victims' being arrested and deported.

Having seen the similarities between trafficking and intimate partner violence, the role of disempowerment and resulting captivity in both, Second Chance has been extending its services to women entrapped in slavery by traffickers. Applying the same principles, and making available to them the same services and resources as those provided to domestic violence victims, we've seen the survivors of trafficking enjoy similar successes.

Our approach also shows great promise for empowering victims in their countries of origin. Given ManPower Group's global presence and existing involvement in helping victims of trafficking, we anticipate the alliance and combined efforts of our organizations will prove especially fruitful in rescuing more people from the enslavement of trafficking.

The laws, policies and practices of some developing countries serve to permit or enable trafficking, sometimes passively, and in some cases by active involvement.

Conditions that have allowed for a proliferation of labor and sex trafficking in Malaysia are described in the U.S. State Department's 2013 *Trafficking in Persons Report*. After noting some of the improvements that have been made in that country, the Report goes on to detail problems that remain.

> As in previous years, NGOs reported referring cases of alleged labor and sex trafficking to the government, but in some instances authorities did not investigate these allegations. NGOs reported that the police and Labor Department officials often failed to investigate complaints of confiscation of passports and travel documents or withholding of wages—especially involving domestic workers—as possible trafficking offenses, and that front-line officers failed to recog-

nize indicators of trafficking and in some cases treated these cases as immigration violations.[41]

Of special interest to the "captivity principle" is the practice of employers to confiscate and hold passports and other travel documents, and to withhold wages. Taking away the ability to travel, and to leave the country, resembles tactics used by domestic batterers to restrict mobility, while preventing victims from terminating the relationship. "Withholding of wages," of course, is directly parallel to the sort of economic abuses we've seen as a major element in the disempowerment of domestic violence victims.

In Malaysia, as in other developing countries, there have been unconfirmed—and perhaps uninvestigated—allegations of official corruption facilitating trafficking.

> The State Department reports alleged that collusion between individual police officers and trafficking offenders led to offenders escaping arrest and punishment. However, there were no confirmed cases of Malaysian officials participating in or facilitating trafficking or trafficking-related crimes, and the Malaysian government took no known steps to prosecute or punish such individuals.[42]

Although Malaysia has been placed on the State Department's "watch list" for failing to comply with minimum standards set forth in the TVPA, in response to international diplomacy and other pressures, the government has shown improvement in recent years. According to the Report, the number of investigations by the Malaysian government into suspected trafficking cases has grown, as has the number of indictments of traffickers. The government has also bolstered training of officials to enforce the 2007 anti-trafficking laws. It has increased the number of shelters for victims, and launched a five-year "national action plan" to address the problem. These are all encouraging signs.

Malaysia is moving in the right direction. But much remains to be done to protect vulnerable populations.

A young girl named Nathalie is illustrative of the atrocities happening now in Malaysia and other countries. Circumstances forced Nathalie to live with a "friend of the family." The "friend" introduced her to a woman who, for reasons she did not understand, made her move to another house. The house that became her new home Nathalie soon learned was a place of prostitution. At the time she arrived, there were a number of girls already living there, some as young as nine. She was forced to obey a woman designated as her "teacher," who trained her how to dance and perform sexual acts to please men.

For many years, Nathalie lived there in appalling conditions, forced to have sex with the men who paid those who enslaved her. She lived under a dictatorship of the "teacher," who was in essence her slave-master, controlling basic survival needs—food, shelter, clothing. In Malaysia, there are thousands of young women and girls suffering under the same sort of intolerable conditions.

To date, political and financial pressures still hold sway over authorities, even in the face of international repercussions. It is widely recognized that in Malaysia and other countries where traffickers proliferate, more robust efforts are needed to change existing laws, and tangible actions to stop these heinous crimes. There must be, for example, more active prosecution and convictions of guilty parties, with meaningful penalties.

In addition to ending government tolerance, and enhancing enforcement and protective measures, I have found in countries around the world an exceptional openness to implementing empowerment programs like Second Chance. Officials and policy-makers with whom I've met are interested in Second Chance because our track record proves that freedom through financial empowerment is possible for survivors and those at risk of forced labor and sex trafficking.

To rescue the countless women and girls who are in situations like Nathalie's, to prevent them from being vulnerable to traffickers in the first place, countries like Malaysia should take measures to facilitate economic opportunity through programs to empower the individual. The Second Chance model, as detailed in Part II, eliminates financial dependency under oppression, captivity, and abusive conditions like those experienced by victims of trafficking.

PART TWO

A SOLUTION THAT LASTS:
Power in the Pursuit of Dreams

As an agency whose clientele are survivors of domestic violence, human trafficking, and other forms of extreme oppression, Second Chance Employment Services is unique both in the goals it sets and in the challenges it must meet to help each client achieve them. While Second Chance is the first employment agency designed specifically to serve people who have been victims of domestic abuse, it is also much more than an employment agency.

To facilitate permanent escape from the tyranny of domestic violence and trafficking, we place our clients in long-term positions that are meaningful to them, with pay and benefits sufficient for financial independence and the flexibility to care for dependent children. To accomplish all this with people who begin with such disadvantages, and to do it all free of charge strikes many as a daunting prospect. I myself have sometimes marveled at the amazing turnarounds of hundreds of survivors' lives.

Clients arrive with many needs and with virtually no self-confidence or belief in their own abilities. Societal misperceptions and unfair prejudice against them are prevalent. The misperceptions are internal as well as external: survivors themselves are often convinced they have nothing of value to offer. For these and other reasons, prospective employers, trying to make rational business decisions, may be inclined to pass them over in favor of candidates who appear to be more stable. How do our clients overcome such obstacles?

To begin with, the success of Second Chance is built on relationships. To accomplish financial independence that leads to permanent escape from domestic violence, Second Chance has established a dynamic network of partnerships, which works in coordination with our own internal resources.

Following our individually tailored employment plans, we perform, or procure from our partners, whatever services are needed: for healing from the trauma of abuse; assessment of talents and possible career interests; preparation for employment; placement in employment; and post-placement tracking and support.

By placing them in work they find fulfilling, in harmony with their career and family aspirations, we facilitate lasting financial security for survivors and their dependents. With new financial and emotional security, Second Chance clients *do not return* to the abusers on whom they formerly depended. They undergo a dramatic transformation from the hopelessness and fear of domestic captivity to financial security and personal fulfillment. Their success is made possible by relationships with others, and by an innovative application of principles of calling and economic empowerment.

CHAPTER 13

The Meaning of Empowerment

Over the past few years, usage of the term "empowerment," in the sense of self-actualization or overcoming oppression, has spread like wildfire though a broad spectrum of disciplines. In public policy, legislation, education, social services, as well as other areas, it would be hard to find a recent discussion without references to empowerment. As with any word that becomes so widely used, there's a danger that by repetition its true meaning may be clouded by cliché, and the value of an important concept diminished. With overuse, the word "empowerment" may lose its power.

Even within the area of domestic violence, there is potential for confusion as different meanings are sometimes assigned to the same term. I hope this chapter will help avoid confusion about the nature of Second Chance's system of financial empowerment.

In 2010, an article about domestic violence appeared in the Cornell Journal of Law and Public Policy with this title: "The Perils of Empowerment." From the title, you might expect the authors to be wary of an organization like mine, which is all about empowerment. But it turns out there is very little in the article at odds with the concepts or methodology of Second Chance, and much that seems to agree. Avoiding misunderstanding and seeming incongruities in this article and others like it, is a matter of defining terms.

"Empowerment" in the article is used mostly to describe what the authors believe was the intention behind laws around the country that give women the right to seek judicial protective orders. The problem, according to the article, is that civil protection orders cannot provide a lasting solution to domestic violence. That idea, of course, is entirely consistent with my own beliefs. The authors explain:

> Granting a battered woman the power to obtain a protective order against her batterer suggests some notion of autonomy, but without also granting her the necessary resources and support, it is a false notion of autonomy given the reality of the impact of violence on women's lives. A woman who is responsible for the care of her children, her home, and the other relationships in her life is by definition not autonomous. Legislatively granting to her something she cannot possibly have will not change that. . . .[43]

The point is not that protective orders should not be available. It is rather that the remedy for temporary protection, without providing financial resources, child care, etc., cannot ultimately liberate or "empower" the victims.

What I call empowerment, however, is designed to rectify the very deficiencies in resources identified in the passage above. The economic empowerment of Second Chance fixes the imbalance of power that prevents lasting freedom from domestic violence. Thus, it is presumably not the sort of "empowerment" the authors would deem "perilous."

The authors suggest that advocates of the empowerment approach to legislation failed to appreciate that the focus on autonomy helps to perpetuate the notion in society that victims are to blame for their own predicament:

> ... from the perspective of those outside the movement, the emphasis on autonomy justified the view that women are responsible for ending the abuse in their lives and that failure to do so is their own fault.[44]

The implication here is again consistent with what I found in the early 2000s. As explained in Part One, I never accepted the prevailing idea that victims stayed in violent relationships as a result of a free-will decision. It was that concept that in my mind contributed to the lack of success in finding a lasting solution, and the very thing that led me to institute the empowerment system of Second Chance.

The same metaphors and allegories used in Part One to illustrate domestic captivity are helpful also here to depict the concept and methods of Second Chance's "empowerment" approach and distinguish it from other approaches.

If domestic captivity is like the invisible electric fence and shock-collar used by dog owners, Second Chance does not try to switch off the electricity. Empowerment at Second Chance means removing the collar! Again, if domestic violence is thought of as a prison camp, we do not concern ourselves with the motives of the jailor, or how the victim's relationship with him might be improved. Rather, in both its urgency and the goal of permanent escape, the empowerment of Second Chance looks more like all-out jail break!

We presuppose no lack of desire on the part of the survivor to be free, so have no need to foster such desires. We do not believe that a victim has to return to the abuser.

Once again, there is the narrative of the wildlife rescue operation. The eagle is first protected, nurtured and healed. Then it is released into its natural habitat on the strength of its own wings. Second Chance orchestrates a host of resources to provide for the survivor's basic material needs (shelter, food, clothing), treatment of injuries physical and psychological, legal protection, childcare, and whatever else is needed.

When our clients are ultimately "released," as it were, it is into a work environment that has been carefully selected to accord with her natural talents, her personal dreams and aspirations—an environment where she can flourish.

The survivor's financial independence as well as her emotional independence are like the two wings of an eagle. These two complementary aspects of her renewed strength will work together to carry her to freedom. So, she rises above the vortex of domestic captivity, no longer susceptible to the gravitational draw of the abuser. The danger of going back is gone. She is empowered to attain lifelong freedom by using her own native strength.

After returning rescued eagles to the wild, some scientists use tracking devices equipped with radio or G.P.S. to track the progress of the birds. One rescuer wrote that his tracking devices revealed "that rehabilitated eagles can do quite well when released into the wild. The birds survived and thrived and have departed for their summer [habitats]."[45] An indispensable aspect our operation is our post-placement tracking system, using a software program specially designed and developed for Second Chance.

From the initial intake, to provision and protection, through healing processes, to placement and post-placement tracking, every element of Second Chance's empowerment program is based on the concepts on which the organization was founded.

CHAPTER 14

The Purpose of Employment and the Employment of Purpose

Second Chance strives to place individuals in suitable positions to the benefit of employer and employee alike. This is nothing novel; it is a basic tenet for any employment agency, and an age-old factor for employers in hiring qualified people for a job. For the employee, a "good fit" is the single most important source not only of job satisfaction and performance but happiness in life beyond the job. My own experiences helped me appreciate that no amount of prestige or money could address the emptiness I felt while not pursuing my calling. Finding a job on Capitol Hill provided me with financial security and a degree of autonomy. But before very long I began to feel that I was in the wrong place, and that I should be doing something else. Because it was not in line with my personal interests, the position that for some was a "dream job" left me feeling unfulfilled. And as long as I felt that way, the financial security was not a firm foundation but a temporary one.

In the case of survivors of abuse, there is a whole other dimension to the importance of finding work that matches one's abilities and passions. It is needed to attain permanent separation from the abuser. A job that is meaningful and fosters the use of one's individual gifts allows for financial autonomy that lasts. Financial autonomy, in turn, is needed for empowerment to break free from the control of the abuser.

If we saw financial empowerment as the only goal, the program would be a failure. To be successful we must have as our focus not only the purpose of employment but also the employment of purpose. A purpose of employment, I've said is financial independence. But what do I mean by employment of purpose?

The French playwright and novelist Honoré de Balzac wrote, "An unfulfilled vocation drains the color from a man's entire existence." Every person has a purpose for being alive. Like Balzac, I believe life's purpose is inseparable from vocation and calling. Whether or not you've been a victim of domestic violence or other severe oppression, you cannot be free or happy unless you are pursing that purpose.

Our government was founded on the idea that a necessary part of being free is the pursuit of happiness. Thomas Jefferson, who made the latter phrase famous, also wrote, "It is neither wealth nor splendor, but tranquility and occupation which give happiness."[46] Happiness is not to be found in a paycheck, but in occupation with tranquility. To have both occupation and tranquility means having more than just a job. It means you're doing what you feel called to do because it is work you have a special ability to do, and it is work you love. Tranquility and occupation in my experience also involves doing the work with passion. It's about pursuing your dreams to fulfill your purpose, the reason you were put on earth, the reason you were given those dreams. Remember, if you have a dream, it is not there by accident. It's there for a reason!

Again, these ideas are universal, by no means limited to survivors of domestic violence. Who can be happy if he or she is not in the right occupation or on a discernible path to the right occupation? How much money you make is ultimately not nearly as important. We see examples all over the news of people who have great wealth, but live in misery.

But for people who have escaped domestic violence, being placed in the wrong occupation, or, as Jefferson might say, being alienated from the pursuit of happiness, has the potential for more immediately harmful and traumatic consequences.

Under a domestic tyranny, victims are conditioned through ritual abuse to accept the lie that they have no purpose outside the dominion and control of the abuser. If the survivor is put in a job with no relevance to the pursuit of her dreams and aspirations, she remains in danger of going back. She is still subject to the vortex. She still lives with the abuser's echo in her mind that she has no reason to live outside his control. She is in danger of leaving the job and going back to the abuser.

This is why at Second Chance, the principles of calling and passion and pursing dreams and aspirations are so critical to our mission. The purpose of employment is fulfilled only when there is also employment of purpose.

The client-survivor's purpose in life must be put to use if the purpose of the job—financial independence—is going to be a reality. Though it might sound fanciful or pie-in-the-sky to some, there is nothing so practical as being able to follow your dreams. In fact, it is indispensable to the success of our system. The survivor's talents, dreams and aspirations must be assessed, so that she may be placed in a position that is tied to use of those talents in pursuit of her personal happiness. If that did not happen, she would likely not find financial independence that lasts. She would remain in danger of returning to the abuser in desperation. The mission of lifelong freedom would not be accomplished, and our empowerment program would be a failure. This would be the case no matter how much the job paid. It would be true if we placed her in a job making a million dollars.

I'm not exaggerating. The great Russian novelist Fyodor Dostoevsky had it right: "[d]eprived of meaningful work, men and women lose their reason for existence...."[47] If you lose the reason for existence, what good is there in gaining all the treasures of the world? This universal truth must never be forgotten in serving survivors of domestic violence and trafficking. If a victim finds herself in a job without meaning or purpose, or at least a pathway to purpose, the abuser's propaganda that she is worthless will seem to her validated. She will likely be subject again to the sway of the domestic tyranny. She will then be drawn back to the despondency, believing there is no hope of escape.

On the other hand, if she is pursuing her calling, doing the kind of work she loves, , even in a job that pays only barely enough to support herself and her children, then she is on her way to permanent escape. As I tell my clients, *Success is not the key to happiness. Happiness is the key to success.* If you truly love what you are doing, you will be both successful and happy. Applying this idea in the context of placement services for victims of domestic violence and trafficking is one of the innovations of Second Chance.

It is no secret that there exists a connection between one's abilities and the sense of true calling. In my own experience, my calling to help survivors has been facilitated by the ability I have in forming lasting relationships and in connecting people with others. It is something that comes naturally to me. As a young girl, I started networking before I knew what networking was. It never occurred to me to form relationships as a means to success. But personal and professional interconnections have been indispensable to the success of Second Chance. They are important in affording access to needed services and fitting employment opportunities for each individual. They are also important in reaching people who have been isolated from society, broken by relationships of the most unwholesome and damaging sort. Forming healthy relationships can be challenging for people whose trust has been so fundamentally violated. But it is a necessary element of their healing and empowerment.

Another ability that was necessary to the Second Chance program was perceiving and sometimes drawing out the talents and dreams of others, and bolstering their confidence in the same by heartfelt encouragement. If I did not believe in the abilities I discern in survivors, they would see through my efforts to embolden and encourage them. Feigned enthusiasm could never serve the purpose of helping them pursue the right occupation or rebuilding the much-needed self-confidence.

People are sometimes surprised that within a short time of making their acquaintance, I'm able to see some particular talent or interest they have. Sometimes it's a passion they've kept secret from even their closest relations—maybe out of fear of criticism or ridicule. Sometimes, it's something the person is not fully conscious of; but after hearing it from someone else, it rings true. A word of heartfelt encouragement from genuine discernment can make a world of difference.

Although I recall friends commenting on this quality even in my childhood, it was not until much later that I understood how it fit with my passion to find a solution for people trapped in domestic violence.

CHAPTER 15

In Practice: Operations of Second Chance

Founded as a non-profit organization in 2001, Second Chance Employment Services is headquartered in Washington, D.C., with satellite offices in Atlanta, New York, Cincinnati, OH, Greenwich, CT, and other locations. Operations are not limited to the activities of the headquarters and satellite offices. Rather, Second Chance has four other divisions, or branches, whose involvement on a client-specific basis is coordinated by the executive and administrative offices. This five-part structure to a large extent grew organically out of the great success of our prototype client, Kara.

As president and founder, my role has been a hands-on collaboration with our partners, as well as getting to know and forming relationships with the clients themselves.

Given the core problems of paralysis and isolation, it is only fitting that a business formed for the client's empowerment should turn on the polar opposite of isolation. Second Chance has incorporated into its very structure a network of diverse people who share a common compassion and interest in empowering survivors of domestic violence and human trafficking.

Character and Structure of the Organization

Second Chance operates with the support and direction of a distinguished Board of Directors. The Board consists of 11 members, including myself. The other ten members are gifted individuals who share compassion for the oppressed who suffer under domestic violence and human trafficking. Another invaluable resource is the Board of Advisors, which includes: former Secretary of State, Madeleine Albright; founder of the *Huffington Post*, Arianna Huffington; former Governor of Virginia, George Allen; former U.S. Senator Bob Dole (Honorary Member); former President and CEO of the Corporation for Public Broadcasting Corporation, Patricia de Stacy Harrison; former CEO, Northrop Grumman Mission Systems, Dr. Ronald Sugar; and other highly regarded leaders in business, public policy, media, arts, entertainment, and other fields.

The human resource professionals at the center of our operations work with each client individually to help her develop a plan tailored to her short- and long-term needs and personal interests, dreams and aspirations. Pursuant to this plan, we coordinate involvement with our four types of partners. Throughout the process we remain actively engaged. We maintain close personal involvement with each client, and are available with ready support, as they go through the process of healing, employment-readiness, and, eventually, placement.

In each of our partnerships, the common goal is preparing the clients for financial independence through the right job. The key is collaboration between Second Chance, the various partners, and the client herself.

The many relationships between the Second Chance executive personnel and our operational partners has helped us grow into a community of support. The Second Chance community consists of many individuals, with diverse socioeconomic and ethnic backgrounds, across a wide spectrum of political beliefs. In our annual fundraising event, the "Last Kiss of Summer," this community, including many survivors now living financially independent, comes together. It is amazing to see how they come from so many diverse backgrounds, drawn together by a common passion for helping people who are hurting and vulnerable, and who can be helped out of hopelessness by the synergy of our combined efforts.

In our day-to-day operations, there must be effective communication and cooperation between the collaborators. During each stage of the process, Second Chance performs ongoing assessments and other internal services as needed, to compliment and sometimes adjust the plan of services provided by our partners, until our client is free of her abuser, and independent.

The Four Branches

The four operational branches are made up of four types of partners: (1) client partners; (2) service partners; (3) job partners; and (4) sponsor partners.

The four corresponding functions of the partners are: (1) client screening and referral; (2) client services; (3) placement; and (4) funding.

Having started out with the informal pledges of support from forty partners, the network has grown to hundreds of entities and individuals, with whom I've formed personal and professional relationships over the years. It is an ever-growing community of diverse individuals. All share the goal to help survivors of human trafficking and domestic violence and their dependents to live the rest of their lives free from abuse.

The partnerships that make up the dynamic network are defined and formalized by memoranda of understanding (MOUs). Each MOU is drafted to fit the shared purposes and objectives of the particular relationship.

Client Partners

Kara's restoration and escape from the tyranny of domestic violence began with a referral from the battered woman's shelter. Had it not been for that referral, I would never have had the opportunity to help her. Out of this experience, the concept of the "client partner" was born. The basic idea is to provide another option for shelters and other client partners to whom victims repair for help. To decrease the risks of survivors' being drawn back into the vortex of domestic violence, shelters and others on the front lines can refer them to Second Chance, knowing our track-record of facilitating permanent separation with no going back.

Any business, in order to operate, must have customers. For Second Chance, the "customers" are survivors of domestic abuse. This basic prerequisite presents special challenges, and not because there's any shortage of victims. A defining characteristic of domestic captivity is the systematic isolation of the victim, including the abusive inhibition of free association and free expression. The restrictions on association are most intense with respect to connections that threaten the abuser's control over the victim. Thus, a challenge to providing our services is finding the women and children who would benefit from them. The very thing we seek to solve–domestic captivity–is also what keeps prospective clients from coming to our doors. This is where our client partners come in.

Client partners are separate entities that provide remedial and emergency services to victims of domestic violence, human trafficking, homeless veterans, and other women in need. Our client partners include: battered women's shelters, social-service agencies, rehabilitative programs, churches and other non-profit organizations, and transitional housing providers. Some of our client partners are listed on Second Chance's website.[48] These are the places that victims can go to in times of crisis, when faced with serious bodily injury and acute emotional trauma. Many are referred to as "safehouses," where victims may be willing to confide in someone about the abuse without incurring violent reaction at home. We have signed MOUs with many agencies and organizations that serve as our client partners.

There are several ways in which client partners are beneficial to Second Chance. As a type of first responder they allow us to help people we otherwise would not be able to reach, and who would not know about our services. With their expert preliminary assessments, they can help ensure that Second Chance is the appropriate place for the person in need, and that our services will be beneficial to them.

By the nature of their services, these entities are regularly in contact with victims of abuse, and are therefore in a position to tell victims about Second Chance, and to make referrals. The client partners have the expertise and resources needed to perform threshold assessments and screening. They are equipped to verify that a prospective referral is a victim of domestic violence, human trafficking, or other oppressive conditions. They evaluate her mental and physical condition, and her readiness for the life-changing program of Second Chance. Referrals from client partners are thus accompanied by a preliminary evaluation and description of the particular needs of the survivor.

Client partners help us by providing opportunities to apply the Second Chance solution to broader societal ills affecting women and children, such as human trafficking and homelessness. Homeless female veterans who were victims of domestic violence, for example, go to agencies seeking aid, but rarely describe their circumstances as the outcome of abuse. Recent studies show that many female veterans have been victims of sexual trauma and abuse. Aware of this phenomenon, our client partners who help with homeless women have been able to learn the abusive histories of homeless veterans and refer them to Second Chance.

From their relationship with Second Chance, client partners benefit in several respects. Services and individuals to whom victims go in times of crisis do the essential and miraculous work of providing safe places, counseling, medical, legal and other help. They hope the victims will not return to the abusers but know that many will. As I mentioned in Part 1, victims taking refuge in shelters may yet remain locked within domestic captivity, on the edge of that invisible vortex that's always drawing them back into the violent relationship.

So, the client partner benefits from playing a key role in our lifelong solution for survivors of domestic violence. Client partner services are designed not to provide a permanent remedy, but are intensely focused on temporary or emergency protection and relief from pain and suffering. The referral to us is something like a doctor who performs an emergency operation, then turns the patient over to a specialist, with reason to expect the referral will facilitate complete recovery from the underlying disease. By partnering with Second Chance, client partners have seen survivors attain the objective of lifelong freedom from domestic violence.

Meaningful employment as a means of preventing victims from going back to abusive relationships, transforming the lives of women and their children, helps those in the business of serving victims of abuse. It saves them from witnessing the cycle of victims going back to the abuser and returning again with further injury, or, the worst of all outcomes, not surviving the next incident of physical brutality.

In addition to playing a part in facilitating a happy outcome, and avoiding the heartbreak of victims returning to the abuser, client partners also benefit from reduced costs resulting from Second Chance. They had learned to expect that many they've cared for will leave and return again with additional injuries, needing additional services. This increases their costs, and reduces resources available to help others in need. So, referring victims to Second Chance results in cost savings for the Client Partner and improved efficiencies. Each time a referred client attains lasting freedom from abuse, the agency can devote more of its resources to helping others in need.

Many shelters have programs to train women in writing resumes, interviewing, and other job-seeking activities. Another way client partners improve efficiencies is by relying on our expertise and resources in workforce solutions. They are then able to concentrate on the work they do best, such as providing temporary safety, assessments, interventions, etc.

Cumulatively, the many alliances between Second Chance and client partners contribute to a more efficient allocation of resources overall in serving survivors. Of course, the consideration that motivates our client partners is not primarily a matter of efficiency. As people who are devoted to serving these vulnerable people, they are enriched in personal, intangible ways on seeing former victims permanently escape a life of terror and pain.

In sum, in the process of providing life-transforming services to battered women, Second Chance also serves those who serve the victims.

Service Partners

Imagine a woman who leaves everything behind to escape violence, and as a result is living in a shelter or is homeless. Her small children have been traumatized by witnessing the attacks against their mother, and are further unsettled by a sudden change of residence.

She has no computer of her own, so any online research or applications must be done when public computers are available. She has no phone, and thus no direct contact information to give to employers. Even if she were able to find a job opening, send a resume, and get an interview, she would have no clothes suitable for the interview, and without transportation of her own, getting to the interview could be a problem. Imagine as a result of attacks by the abuser, several teeth are missing, or her jaw has been knocked out of line, or her face is scared from years of brutality.

How could she hope to present herself with the necessary poise and self-assuredness to convince an employer to hire her? The obstacles to finding a job are at best discouraging.

In fact, for a woman in such a predicament, the chances of obtaining employment are pretty much zero. On the one hand, leaving the abuser has left her facing a real possibility of destitution. On the other hand stands the abuser, ready to take her back and provide for basic material needs. But, of course, going back would mean putting her life at risk, subjecting herself to verbal abuse and vicious physical assaults, and subjecting her children to further psychological trauma.

This woman we are imagining is no fiction. In fact, women referred by our client partners come to Second Chance in situations just like hers. They stand at the edge of that vortex of his control, poised to be swept with her children back into the spiraling arms of captivity and death that is domestic violence.

Physical, verbal, and economic abuses have conspired to impart the propaganda that the victim has no worth or meaning outside her relationship to the batterer, that she can't survive without his providence. And as a practical matter, without a real solution that leads to a permanent escape, she has no hope of rising above the swirling currents. As long as she remains under this gravitational pull, she is in danger of going back. And it's a matter of life and death.

After becoming a client of Second Chance, that powerful vortex is counteracted by the more powerful network of resources we call our "service partners." It's a network that has been growing over the years through personal and professional relationships, and is made up of many compassionate specialists who have an amazing array of experience and talent. They come from many disciplines and donate a wide range of goods and services in their areas of expertise.

Through this extensive network we are able to provide for: physical safety and protection; basic survival; medical treatment for physical injuries; child care; counseling for emotional damage and depression; assistance with our own internal assessments of employment interests and aptitudes; training for interviews and resume-writing; transportation; and many other needs.

The panoply of services is a reflection of the multifaceted and complex nature of issues confronting victims of domestic abuse. No single entity or profession could address all the issues confronted by the diversity of personalities and circumstances that we encounter. There are also many variations in the nature of their injuries and deprivations.

Our service partners include: medical doctors; lawyers; psychologists; child care providers; hotels and other providers of temporary housing; dentists; and even a reconstructive surgeon who provides free reconstructive services to domestic violence victims.

Other partners provide transportation for clients. Companies and agencies involved in transportation donate fare cards. There are volunteers who drive clients to interviews or their job. We will give clients tickets and tokens for public transportation, if needed.

Professional hair stylists, clothing companies and others from cosmetic and fashion industries provide professional clothing, and make-up, as these are essential for interviewing and working in a professional environment.

Our service partners are dedicated and talented people, who provide top-quality goods and services, free of charge. In addition to being exceptionally well qualified in their particular fields, Service Partners are also compassionate people, who genuinely care about those in need. The combination of talent and empathy translates to a consistent level of care in keeping with our high standards. Without question, the unprecedented record of success of our clients owes much to the service partners' generous contributions of time, talent and expertise.

The terms of the MOUs between Second Chance and the service partners depend on the type of service needed and the particular partner. From time to time, we encounter clients whose needs go beyond the expertise of service partners in the network. In those cases, Second Chance finds (often with the assistance of the existing network) the resources required to solve the issue. Service partners make up a dynamic network that grows to expand the geographical reach as well as the types of services provided.

As in all our partnerships, the arrangement is mutually beneficial to both parties to the MOU. How do service partners benefit? For one thing, they have found the ancient wisdom is true: giving sacrificially is a source of great happiness. They see how donating their gifts makes a real contribution towards helping women and their children escape intolerable conditions, and towards transforming their lives from darkness to light. This is what keeps service partners coming back again and again to offer their services to Second Chance clients. Service partners are also able to form friendships and professional networks with others who share similar passion for helping vulnerable people in need.

A unique aspect of the system lies in the carefully orchestrated use of these many services to address the particular needs of each individual client. For each client, the services of a specially tailored selection of service partners are arranged following an individual employment plan. (As explained in the discussion of "Internal Resources," the employment plan is developed by our internal human resources experts in consultation with and other experts and the client). The purpose is to begin the process of counteracting the captivity of domestic tyranny, by meeting the individual's needs and preparing her for appropriate employment.

Depending on the circumstances, we may begin by connecting a client to a service partner to provide housing, food or clothing to address material needs. A service partner who is a doctor may be called in to address medical needs of the victim and her children. We may introduce her to another service partner able to help redress psychological harm caused by a particular kind of mistreatment, and, at the appropriate time, to professionals who conduct mock job interviews, provide help with drafting resumes, services for training in various ways to become more employable, and whatever other services are needed to help her overcome the specific obstacles in her journey out of captivity.

An example of an important service is the one provided by our service partner, Verizon Communications. Through its "Hope Line" program, Verizon furnishes to Second Chance clients free cell phones pre-loaded with 3,000 minutes per year. The phones give them a means of reaching out for help in an emergency that they otherwise would not have. It also provides a way for prospective employers to contact clients directly. It is vitally important for them to have a line unknown to the abuser, free from his control.

Cosmetic needs arising from physical attacks pose a unique challenge for victims of domestic violence seeking employment. Some may wonder if these cosmetic issues are too trivial or superficial to merit attention. In fact, cosmetic and reconstructive services have been critical to many of our clients. As anyone who has looked for a job knows, appearances and first impressions during the interview stage are critical. For a victim of battering, normal concerns about appearance are magnified, as the marks of abuse can affect both appearance and behavior during interviews.

Bruises, lacerations, burns, and other visible injuries; or the outward signs of unseen injuries like broken bones: these common effects of domestic violence impact the willingness of even the most sympathetic employers to hire victims of violence.

The impact of service partners like the reconstructive surgeon has been miraculous. For example, Mary, one of my first clients had been ferociously attacked by her abuser, leaving her with broken teeth and conspicuous facial scars. We began by helping her with, among other things, preparing a competitive resume, and with interview skills. Sending her resume to various employers succeeded in landing her several job interviews. But none of those interviewers resulted in an offer. The reason was no secret. She was greatly disadvantaged by the marks of physical abuse.

Then our service partner, Dr. Ronald Perlman, performed surgery on Mary to repair the facial scars. Another service partner, dental surgeon, Kevin Ryan, DDS, performed reconstructive dental surgery and replaced missing teeth. The success of these services was instantaneous. On Mary's first post-surgery interview, she was offered a full-time job with benefits.

Another client who benefited from the service partner described her experience as follows:

> I was a victim of physical abuse, which had left me with scars on my face. I was very self-conscious and humiliated because of my scars, and every time I [looked] into the mirror, I was reminded of the episodes [that caused them]. . . . I felt . . . everyone was staring at that scar, and found it very hard to maintain eye contact. . . .

> . . . [After cosmetic surgery donated by Second Chance's service partner]: I am feeling tremendous . . . not only is my physical reminder of the violence gone, but . . . with the newly found love and trust that has been shown to me unconditionally, I was able to be healed of my psychological [wounds] and rediscover my self-esteem. . .

As this testimony implies, the emotional injuries caused from the physical manifestations of abuse contribute to the victim's disadvantage in getting a job.

The damage to the victim's physical appearance, and the secondary impact to her emotional state, combines to impose barriers to employment that seem, and may be, insurmountable. Because the physical marks of domestic violence are one of the elements that contribute to the isolation and disempower the victim, we view this aspect of the woman's condition as anything but trivial. Service partners who donate their special services to redress such injuries are extremely important to the program.

Other service partners in the medical field include Robert Adamski, a superb psychologist; and outstanding dentists, such as Alona Bauer, D.D.S., Claudia Cotca, D.D.S. and Kevin Ryan, D.D.S.

One of our clients from Boston was referred to service partner Tina Alster, M.D., a brilliant dermatologist, who diagnosed and treated the client for melanoma. Melanoma is a form of skin cancer that is often fatal unless treated promptly. Thanks to Dr. Alster, the cancer was caught early and completely removed.

From various areas of the fashion and cosmetic industry, we have as partners other superbly skilled professionals. Some have been makeup artists and hair stylists for well-known personalities in television and other media. The amazingly talented stylists, Katy Ghirardo and Benjamin Duboeuf, at Christophe Salon, whose regular clientele include Hollywood celebrities, news and other media personalities, generously donate their time and talent to Second Chance clients, serving 10 clients per week! Our clients are given three complete interview outfits, including accessories, shoes, and often coats as well. Once they are employed, they can return to us for a full week of professional clothing. These arrangements are possible thanks to the generous donations of service partners who donate clothing. Donations of clothing are made by charities, clothing stores, and major corporations in the fashion and apparel industries, including Macy's, Bloomingdale's, Sax Fifth Avenue, Nordstrom. Based on the commitment of these outstanding service partners, our job partners are assured that, if hired, our clients will have appropriate clothing to wear to work.

Another extraordinary service partner is an obstetrician, who is highly regarded in his profession. He has provided prenatal care and even delivered the babies of Second Chance clients. We have also partnered with attorneys from top firms in Washington, DC, who provide pro bono legal services. They help us get temporary restraining orders against the batterers; ensure our clients and partners are in compliance with applicable laws and regulations; and provide outstanding assistance with legislative and policy issues, as in our success in passing the Second Chance provision of the newly amended VAWA with the assistance of Arent Fox.

Clients who are not fluent in English can present special challenges. Language in these cases is a major barrier to getting and keeping a job. Perpetrators of domestic violence and human trafficking will affirmatively prevent their victims from learning English. For example, they stop them from taking English as a Second Language (ESL) classes. Her inability to speak English greatly enhances his power over her. It is also a major obstacle to finding employment. English is not only the language necessary for most jobs, it is also needed to understand information and counseling for those trapped in domestic violence. For these reasons, I've always insisted that ESL training must be provided for our clients who are not fluent in English.

With the orchestrated provision of goods and services from our service partners, the woman described above has a chance. The services prepare her for interviewing and for success in the workplace. They help counteract the power of the abuser that would draw her back into the destructive relationship. We and our partners are committed to arrange for services to overcome whatever stands in the way of her permanent escape.

In this chapter, I am able to mention only a small percentage of our many outstanding service partners. To include them all would require a separate book!

Job Partners

Businesses that enter into an alliance with Second Chance and pledge their willingness to consider our clients for employment, we call "job partners." As service partners address a multiplicity of needs to empower survivor-clients to attain the goal of lifelong freedom, job partners are the branch where aspirations turn to reality.

In addition to the intangible benefits of helping people in need, job partners stand to benefit financially. For one thing, job partners obtain top-notch employment services free of charge, without the substantial fees charged by for-profit agencies. In terms of academic and professional background, years of practical experience, and effectiveness in providing workplace solutions, Second Chance is second to none. Moreover, our clients have an even more compelling motive to succeed in their job than other candidates. For them, it is a means to escape the intolerable, life-threatening conditions of domestic violence.

In spite of these potential benefits to job partners, given the personal challenges associated with victims of domestic violence and trafficking, a business may be reluctant at first to become a job partner. When economic conditions make finding employment difficult for just about everyone (certainly the case at the time I'm writing this book), employers can be highly selective in hiring. Our competitors, for-profit employment agencies, are presumably sending candidates who have no known background of abuse. So, you might get the idea that Second Chance has to relax its standards in selecting prospective employers. Nothing could be further from the truth.

As indicated on the Second Chance website, our job partners include some of the most competitive highly regarded employers in the country, businesses like Booz Allen Hamilton, Macy's, IBM, Hilton Hotels, SunTrust Bank, George Washington University Hospital, and many others.[49]

Second Chance has exceptionally high standards for selecting businesses to become job partners. We are interested only in employers that have the potential to advance the founding purposes of Second Chance. Also, because my business grew out of compassion for the victims of domestic abuse, and because we devote ourselves to building relationships with people who have been subjected to unspeakable brutality, I am personally committed to ensuring that we place them in healthy working environments. We look for employers who show the attributes of one who would always treat employees with dignity. We must be convinced that people to whom my clients would report have a capacity to value the unique gifts of every individual, and to appreciate and cultivate those gifts. We are especially interested in companies that foster a culture of encouragement among their employees, and relationships of mutual respect and trust.

Prospective employers must be able to provide a stable work environment and fair terms of employment. Typically, they must allow for advancement, either within the company, or with job training and experience that would allow for the employee to pursue her dreams. In view of our core mission, the partners are usually able to offer long-term, meaningful employment, and pay enough for financial independence. For clients who may benefit from temporary positions to smooth a transition to financial independence, we occasionally seek job partners with openings for temporary or part-time positions.

Some job partners also function as service partners. For example, they supplement Second Chance's in-house human resource functions, from the invaluable perspective of a potential employer. They provide additional training for clients on resume-writing, interviewing, and consultation on self-presentation. Some have even agreed to give us what we call "first class preference." This means, for appropriate job openings, they put Second Chance resumes on the top of the pile and consider them first.

Of course, establishing solid relationships between Second Chance and our job partners is not a one-way street. We must also work hard to earn the confidence of existing and prospective job partners.

In addition to financial advantages to partnering with Second Chance, those who form a job partner alliance are also motivated by compassion. Job partners have a heart for helping survivors of domestic violence and trafficking. They empathize with wounded people who may be shunned by other employers, and who face considerable challenges to attain financial independence for themselves and their children. Nevertheless, taking the initial step to sign an MOU with Second Chance takes courage.

The very circumstances that move business leaders to compassion must also give them pause. They may wonder, will psychological and physical injuries inhibit the survivor's ability to become a productive employee? Will those elements render her less productive than other applicants? They may even worry about the possibility of former abusers threatening their businesses and other employees.

So, in pledging their willingness to consider Second Chance candidates, prospective job partners may see themselves as taking a larger risk than they would by hiring other candidates. Compassion and empathy, and the aforementioned financial advantage, may prompt businesses to open their doors, and their ears, to a possibility; but successful businesses understand that being compassionate does not mean being foolhardy.

After all, the greater their success in business, the more resources they have available to extend compassion to people in need. Job partners must be able to trust that Second Chance will refer candidates with the potential to contribute value that equals or surpasses the value added by any other employee.

In some ways, the process of winning and keeping our job partners' trust has become easier over time, as a result of our former clients' remarkable successes, and their records of strong performance in the workplace. These successes consistently show the effectiveness of the Second Chance system. A strong track record is important. But the past is not always enough to maintain the level of confidence needed to keep ongoing relationships, or attract new job partners. Every new hire must also be a prudent business decision.

The involvement of people in the other three branches of Second Chance is an important factor in allaying any initial concerns of our job partners. They recognize the strength of our client partners in performing initial assessments; the extensive network of service partners to address the survivor's needs; and our internal monitoring and expertise in human resources to ensure they are prepared and qualified for the opening, and highly motivated to succeed. Another important consideration for job partners is that we and all of our partners remain involved for as long as services our needed, in the event any post-placement issues arise.

Another objective is to build a global network for survivors of domestic abuse anywhere it occurs. In the process, a growing number of businesses and communities will come to appreciate more fully the burdens imposed on them by domestic violence and trafficking, and, at the same time, the contributions of real value the survivors have to offer.

Alliance with ManPower Group

While most of our job partners are prospective employers, we are open to other kinds of relationships that stand to advance our system of permanent liberation for survivors of domestic violence. A recent example is our alliance with Manpower Group, one of the world's largest employment service organizations and a world-leader in human resources and workforce solutions. The $22 billion dollar company also has a long history of implementing effective solutions for disadvantaged individuals around the globe. David Arkless, Manpower Group's President of Corporate and Government Affairs, was named President of the Board of End Human Trafficking Now (EHTN), in

July 2011. ManPower Group is extensively involved in the fight to combat human trafficking.

To expand the reach of employment services to victims of human trafficking and domestic violence, Second Chance and Manpower Group have signed a Memorandum of Understanding, reflecting our intention to pool the respective strengths of the two organizations. Beginning with pilot locations in the United States, Second Chance now has the potential to expand to any of the 82 countries and territories where Manpower operates. Our partnership with them allows us to combine resources with a world leader in the industry, and benefit from their networks and their geographical reach, thus opening unique opportunities to replicate and scale our services in other locations domestically and internationally.

Working together, Manpower Group and Second Chance will deploy our unique and complementary innovations and networks for a common purpose: to bring meaningful, sustainable employment, financial independence, and hope, to thousands of additional women.

Partners with Multiple Functions

Some of Second Chance partners work with us in more than one capacity. Macy's, for example, has been actively engaged with Second Chance as a job partner, a service partner and a sponsor. Macy's management takes its social responsibility very seriously, as I've learned first-hand. The senior executives and other personnel I've worked with at Macy's have acted with a depth of understanding and the kind of tenacious engagement that have been enormously important to helping Second Chance clients. I've encountered at Macy's a corporate culture of compassion and integrity, and a willingness to extend a helping hand to give vulnerable people a second chance.

Our partnership with Macy's began in 2005, when the vice president of Human Resources agreed to help one our clients, whom I'll call Rosa. Rosa was a young Hispanic woman who was being repeatedly battered by her husband. With her life in danger, she took refuge with her three young children in the House of Ruth shelter in Washington. House of Ruth, one of our client partners, then referred Rosa to Second Chance.

Rosa had suffered serious physical and psychological wounds. Low self-esteem was a major obstacle to getting a job. Macy's Human Resources set up an interview for her. They also provided clothing and jewelry for her to wear to the interview. (Macy's thereafter became a regular contributor of wardrobes for use by our clients in interviews). The business attire and accessories, along with other steps we'd taken, were effective to help improve Rosa's self-confidence. Her interview was successful. Macy's hired Rosa for a retail sales position at Macy's store in Arlington, Virginia. This position provided Rosa with a steady income with benefits in a wholesome and stable work environment.

For Rosa, the job at Macy's made all the difference. It allowed her to become financially independent without having to depend on the violent spouse. It also marked the beginning of a fulfilling career, the key to ensuring that she and her children would never return to the abusive relationship.

On its website, Macy's sums up its attitude towards social responsibility in five words: "actions speak louder than words." Rosa's experience shows how Macy's truly lives up to its commitment to act. Rosa is not an isolated case, but an example of the company's continuous outreach with life-changing results. Dedicated partners like Macy's are essential to many favorable outcomes of the Second Chance program.

Sponsor Partners

Second Chance could not function without the financial support of sponsor partners, whose generous donations help pay for administrative and operational costs. Sponsors include individuals and businesses that experience the joy of charitable giving to a reliable, systematic way of emancipating survivors.

In addition to sponsor partnerships, public investment has been helpful during an economic downturn to allow Second Chance to continue providing services of the highest quality.

Recently, Second Chance's reach and effectiveness has been expanded through legislative authorization of additional funds. The reenactment of the Violence Against Woman Act, with the Second Chance provision, for the first time specifically authorizes allocation of funds to non-profit organizations providing employment services and employment retention counseling. The purpose of the provision, as discussed in Chapter 17, is to improve the reach of Second Chance and other organizations that provide this kind of service, such as those that wish to follow our business model.

Notwithstanding the potential for increased public funding, the most important source will always be private giving. Those who donate to Second Chance, benefit from a higher level of awareness and sometimes direct involvement in work on behalf of victims of violent domestic relationships. Second Chance's W-track system gives accountability to our contributors, reliably detailing how the money is used, what services are provided, and the results.

At our annual fundraising event, one our former clients, Philomena, gave an account of her experiences as a victim of violence and her liberation through Second Chance. At the end of her speech, she said, "I want to thank all of you who are here tonight! You are the supporters that make the work of Second Chance possible. Without your contributions, I really don't know where my children and I would be today." The statement is representative of the gratitude of so many whose lives have been transformed through the Second Chance program.

Our Internal Program

If the four types of partners are thought of as a wheel, then at its hub is Second Chance's executive and administrative offices.

The Importance of Relationships

Relationships between Second Chance and the survivors, between the survivors and our partners, between the partners and Second Chance:

these relationships are an important component of the antidote to the brokenness and captivity caused by the destructive relationships.

If not for relationships between Second Chance and our partners, and the shared belief that serving the needs of others is a source of great fulfillment, the program would never work. When our clients find themselves among people seeking to help them, with the clients' best interests at heart, a healthy model for restoring trust and confidence is formed.

Upon Referral From Client Partner

When we meet with a person referred by a client partner we explain the processes of Second Chance, and the kinds of services available. We offer her the option of becoming a client of Second Chance. In making the offer we convey our vision for her life: nothing less than permanent freedom from domestic violence. That, after all, is the core mission of Second Chance. It is part of what makes Second Chance unique.

The importance of instilling self-confidence in victims of domestic abuse cannot be overstated. The process of restoring self-esteem may need to be gradual and gentle, but it cannot be started to soon. I don't know how I or my staff could begin the process without believing in the solution ourselves. Based in part on the many Second Chance clients who have left domestic violence and trafficking, and never returned, I never doubt that a newly referred victim can be empowered to follow the same success in her own unique way.

If I sound confident, it's because I know the system works! In fact, when I speak with clients and prospective clients, it would be impossible for me to hide my confidence in them. The good news: confidence is contagious!

In addition to the contagious confidence, our approach grows out of sincere appreciation for the uniqueness and immeasurable worth of each individual—the opposite of the beliefs inculcated under the tyranny of domestic abuse. With people whose trust has been deeply violated, it is imperative from the outset to foster a relationship of mutual trust, with gentleness and respect. In the first meeting with a prospective client, and in all later interactions, we operate in an atmosphere of compassion and empathy, and above all making it clear to victims that our role is not to judge them.

The Employment Plan

If a woman agrees to become a Second Chance client, the next step is to undertake an in-depth assessment of her needs. We supplement the preliminary assessment done by the client partner with our own evaluation of her condition and needs; educational background; training and experience; special talents, abilities, interests and passions. Based on these assessments of each client, we develop a preliminary plan to meet short- and long-term needs. Though we call it the "employment plan," many steps relate to employment only indirectly. The plan is a step-by-step, flexible process that often begins with medical and legal services, and includes completion of training programs recommended or started by client partners.

The plan is designed to help them heal and grow in preparation for interview and placement with a job partner. Throughout the execution of the plan, Second chance stays actively involved. We determine the service partners needed to meet the specific needs, with the right service, at the appropriate time. For example, we coordinate the timing of services in consultation with the service partners and the client, and arrange for communications as needed between various service partners.

The plans may change, and often do, as we go along, to adapt to additional needs as they arise, to take into account interests and abilities that may not have been known at the time of the assessments, and, of course, to address challenges and obstacles that invariably appear along the way. Knowing how domestic tyranny crushes the spirit and represses goals and dreams, it is important to remain open to new information coming to light as our relationship with the client develops and she learns to trust us. We are especially interested in learning about their dreams and finding ways to make them come true.

In developing the employment plan, we strive to create an environment in which the client feels safe to disagree with our recommendations and referrals, to express herself openly. In the context of the service and job partner referrals, we recognize that our ideas about logistical and substantive aspects of the plan may differ from the client's plans. As we have seen, a domestic tyranny inhibits the victim's freedom to express herself. Unpredictable, violent responses to any expression have conditioned some women to stay silent about their own views. It's not surprising, therefore, if she does not readily or openly express disagreement with our plan of action.

Our responsibility is to be sensitive to indications that the client has reservations about any aspect of the plan, and to make adjustments as appropriate. We bear in mind the impact abuse has had on her psyche, her self-confidence, her ability to express herself. But the client must play a role in establishing her employment plan. She is often in the best position to identify problems with our plan. Moreover, by giving her an active role in determining the way forward, we are already allowing her to appreciate her own importance and value in determining her own destiny.

This does not mean we shy away from giving frank advice. Speaking honestly with gentleness strengthens the relationships and is essential to serving the client's best interests. But we work proactively to assure clients understand that Second Chance is their advocate, not their judge; and that our advice and actions are grounded in experience and knowledge, and grow out of genuine desire for their highest good. Of course, none of this will be persuasive if the client does not trust us. So, again the importance of trust is paramount. If a client didn't trust us, she would be much less likely to follow the employment plan.

The clients depend on us to walk with them, physically, and emotionally through the process of healing. We do this for as long as it takes for broken wings to heal. Gradually their natural strength is restored and they begin to do it on their own. Careful discernment is needed to gauge how much personal assistance each individual requires at each step along the way.

Although every employment plan is unique, and there is limitless variety from one to the next, all plans share one thing in common. All are developed with constant consideration of our mission and ultimate purpose. So, as we make the plans for provision of goods and services, for training in job-seeking and job-readiness, and for placement in the right job, it's important to bear in mind that each of these steps is a means to the end, not the end itself.

In light of what I've called the "employment of purpose," and the critical importance of calling and the pursuit of dreams, an empowerment system like ours benefits from expertise in discerning unique qualities and strengths in others. It must be remembered, especially in the early stages, that native strengths and interests have been repressed by abuse. From the outset while she receives treatment needed for physical and psychological injuries to heal, we are looking for ways to help her native power and beauty to blossom.

Another important resource of our internal program is the building of the network. Interpersonal skills, whether they come naturally or are learned, would seem to be essential in building a network of this kind.

Post-Placement Support

An important part of our program, and a pledge to job partners, is continued support as needed after placement. We are committed to ensuring the satisfaction of the job partner with our client and to the success of the client in her job. So, we provide post-placement support for as long as it is needed.

A good example of post-placement support may be seen in the case of Maria, whose story is told in more detail in Chapter 16. After we placed Maria in a job she had been promoted to team leader. But about a year after she took the job, she called our office in tears. It was the first time she had been in a leadership position and now she found herself unable to resolve certain conflicts with fellow team members and superiors. Our staff worked with both Maria and her superiors to resolve the problem. We arranged for Maria to learn conflict-resolution skills, which she then applied to her situation. Maria kept her job and continued to excel.

Post-placement support is important to our goals as well, given our focus on long-term careers for financial stability.

W-Track: A Proven Tracking System

Second Chance's services do not end upon placement. Rather, we continue to monitor our client's progress to ensure they are meeting their goals and that the job partners who hire them are entirely satisfied. To fulfill this commitment to clients and our network of partners, we have developed our own tracking software program, known as "W-Track."

W-Track, developed in 2001 in collaboration with IT experts from IBM, was, as far as we know, the first web-based system in America for monitoring and reporting community services programs. The system meets federal reporting requirements for such programs. In 2007, the U.S. Department of Labor selected W-track as a national pilot for monitoring grantee services. A year later, the Labor Department again licensed W-track for regional conferences on documenting and reporting grantee programs. In 2008, the Justice Department selected W-track for a project providing technical assistance to transitional housing grantees.

The system is programed to gather and store data in an internally searchable database with detailed information relating to clients' progress, and to maintain contact with each client for two years after she has been placed in a permanent position. It operates 24 hours a day, seven days a week.

W-Track is an indispensable tool for post-placement tracking and support. It also allows us to document and verify our rates of success in facilitating financial independence and permanent separation from domestic abusers. With W-Track, Second Chance is able to monitor client progress and provide reports in detail sufficient to verify the effectiveness of our services on an individual basis, and system-wide.

This type of tracking and reporting is crucial to demonstrate to our support partners, and to prospective donors and granting entities, the effectiveness of our program. The reports generated through W-Track are also important to job partners, client partners and service partners.

In addition to measuring the success of Second Chance, and individual clients, W-Track also helps us assess the effectiveness of the services provided in each case. We begin using W-Track from the initial intake, and with it track services provided to each client and by each partner.

The Spinning Wheel: Turning Straw to Gold
Someone once compared Second Chance to the magic spinning wheel in the fairy tale that turns straw into gold. I think what he meant was that we take in a person who is perceived as having nothing of value to offer; she moves around a wheel, from client partners to service partners to job partners, and in the end, to the surprise and delight of many, becomes a person of great value to her community.

It is a collaborative effort that helps solve the daunting challenges confronting survivors of domestic violence and trafficking. Profound sacrifices are made by many—people who trust us with referrals, volunteer their expert services, take risks to hire survivors, donate their own money, and exercise judgment in administering public and private grants: all of these activities are evidence of the goodness of the cause and the trustworthiness of the method.

The various parts of our operations generate synergy. The outstanding work of our service partners adds to the confidence of prospective employers—our job partners and those who might join as such. By the same token, the commitment of job partners to the survivors, with a history of providing long-term stable employment with good pay and benefits, gives a powerful incentive to "first responders," if you will, to make referrals and become our client partners. The growth in referrals is another barometer of trust that the program leads to permanent release from the intractable problem of domestic violence. That trust adds to the sense of purpose and enthusiasm of service partners as they play a key role in making it happen. Client partners, service partners, job partners, acting and interacting, with documented success, together inspire sponsor partners to provide funding through donations and grants, knowing that the money is being used effectively to accomplish the stated mission.

With the uncompensated leadership of a distinguished Board of Directors and Board of Advisors, we coordinate the activities of all four branches and contribute expertise of our own to compliment the others. Trust inspires trust, action leads to action, in this dynamic and diverse community of highly talented, respected and dedicated partners. From the hub of activity, with many moving parts in view, it is possible, after all, to see a great wheel turning, almost by magic, to change straw into gold.

There is a deeper secret to this alchemy. The secret is there really is no magic. What some thought was worthless straw, the victim of domestic violence or human trafficking, was never straw to begin with. From the beginning, she was always gold.

CHAPTER 16

Mounting Up on Wings: True Stories of Lasting Freedom

Like the eagle restored, hundreds of women have left behind their former brokenness forever. The successes recounted below are representative of many happy outcomes with the help of Second Chance and our network of partners. The narratives are based on interviews with the clients, responses to our survey questions, statements by clients, and notes taken by me and my staff.

Anna

Anna was married to a partner of a large law firm in Washington, D.C. He abused her severely for many years. There were times when he tied her to a household fixture and left her there for days to keep her imprisoned.

After Anna's referral to Second Chance, we coordinated services she needed for her protection, physical and emotional healing, and preparation for employment. Initially, she was hired by one of our job partners to work as an administrative assistant. It was a steady job in a stable environment that allowed her to support herself.

We learned that Anna's dream was to be a professional artist. When I saw one of her paintings, I said, you do *not* want to be an artist. You *are* an artist! I could not believe my eyes. It was breathtaking. But years of abuse had left her so depressed and dejected that she no longer appreciated how exceptional her talent was, or no longer cared.

But now I saw her passion as an artist was every bit as intense as the passion that drove me to help survivors like her. Of course, I could not let her give up on her dream. I had to find a way to get her work in front of people who would promote her work.

My network of friends and professional connections finally led me to Katherine Wood, Board member of the National Museum of Women in the Arts in Washington, D.C. I arranged a meeting with her and took one of Anna's paintings. I showed it to the curator and she agreed that it was exceptional. She arranged an exhibition of Anna's paintings at the museum.

This precious woman had been treated with such violent hatred and contempt for so many years that she had come to regard herself as less than worthless. Now she could hardly believe that her dream of long ago was coming true, and that her own paintings were actually on display at a national museum. And that was just the beginning. Anna's work is now being shown at museums around the world!

Diane

Diane's narrative continues from Part One.

"Ludy Green believed in me before I could believe in myself." This is what Diane said in a speech she prepared for a fundraising event. From my perspective, that was no big deal. What I found remarkable was that she did *not* see her own potential. But of course I recognized her self-abasement as a common effect of domestic abuse.

After Diane moved out of her husband's house, for the reasons described in her story, she was still subject to the strong pull of his control that had grown over the course of more than a decade. She had left him before and had been drawn back to live with him again. This was her condition when she was referred to Second Chance.

At my suggestion, she worked as a volunteer at Second Chance. It gave her some stability and allowed me to get to know her and her circumstances.

At the same time, when she was feeling helpless and afraid, she learned about what Second Chance had done for other victims. We became friends, and she told me her "true calling in life."

At the fundraiser, Diane said, "It was at that point that my spirit began to revive. I found a determination to stay out of the relationship [with my husband]."

Diane had immediately impressed me as very bright and articulate, a woman of enormous talent. Eventually, she told me of her lifelong interest in dermatology and skin care. I had an opportunity to introduce Diane to one of our supporters who is in show business. As a result of that connection Diane was hired as a make-up artist for celebrities. From there she went on to work for a major pharmaceutical company and eventually developed and marketed skin care products of her own. "My self-confidence was returning, in a way I had never before felt. My old insecurities about my husband's status, my own significance, were dissolving away. Instead of seeking false security through him, I was finding true security in using my own God-given talents."

Diane has attained a level of personal and financial success beyond her dreams. The financial and emotional independence allowed her separate permanently from the abusive spouse and never return.

She believes that without Second Chance's help, sooner or later her husband would have killed her. She came to Second Chance doubting she would survive, and in a relatively short period of time she was flourishing.

Angel (Victim of Human Trafficking)

Originally from Mali, Angel had been working as a model in African countries and other locations around the world. She was about 19 when an older man convinced her to join his company with promises of better work. He was actually a sex trafficker. He pretended to fall in love with her and deceived her with promises of a life together with economic security. After moving to the United States, she found herself in a culture that was very strange to her, where she did not speak the language and was entirely dependent on the man for her material needs. He used the coercive tactics of sex traffickers to force her into prostitution. To make her compliant, he threatened and beat her, forced her to go without food, plied her with alcohol, and punished her when she did not make enough money.

In 2006, Angel was referred to Second Chance by a non-profit organization known as the Polaris Project. When she came to us she was pregnant, and we connected her with a service partner, an obstetrician who provided prenatal care and delivered her child. Other partners, Sisters of Charity, and WEAVE, respectively, provided decent housing and pro bono legal services. With the assistance of Second Chance and our connections with many universities and colleges, Angel was admitted with a scholarship to Southeastern University in Washington, DC. She graduated in May 2011 with a major in financing, and is presently working as a financial assistant at Cardinal Bank, a Second Chance job partner.

Myra (Continued from Part One)

Myra was referred to our office by a client partner whose evaluation indicated the need for psychological healing. Our service partner, psychologist Robert Adamski, provided counseling services, as we worked with her to improve her resume, coached her to prepare for job interviews, provided clothing, and referred her to other service partners for makeup, and hair-styling services. As she got back on her feet emotionally, and was in other ways empowered for financial and emotional independence, it turned out to be relatively easy to find meaningful work for Myra, in part because she had a strong background already.

Latisha

Latisha's spouse was violently abusive and nearly killed her by poisoning her food. Through Second Chance, she was hired by the World Bank, where she has a well-paying job that has allowed her to be financially independent. Latisha, who is pursuing her musical aspirations, told her story at a fundraising event for Second Chance:

"Years ago I came to this country as the wife of a foreign diplomat. I thought I had married the most wonderful man. He was talented and powerful. He moved in the right circles.

"But in my house I was mistreated. My husband abused me and beat me. He was very unhappy about my decision to take classes, or even get better on computers. He said I didn't need to learn anything new. One day when I came home from school, he started to beat me and insult me in front of our children, and he said my place was to stay home and cook and have babies.

"To punish me, he refused to buy food or clothes. The ladies in my church helped me with small amounts of money to buy lotion, toothpaste and other stuff.

"When the church bought me food, my husband threw it in the trash can and poured milk in the sink.

"My husband was beating me when I was pregnant with my daughter. I thought he would stop beating me because I was carrying his child. Instead, it got worse, and he started withholding money from me. So I was realizing then how important it was for me to develop skills and go to work.

"After my daughter was born, my husband tried to kill me by poisoning my food. I lay in the hospital bed, clinging to life but not knowing what life had in store for me, I decided I had to take my children and escape. But I had nowhere to go.

"After I left, my husband was threatening to kill me, and of course I knew he would do it. So for three years, my children and I went from shelter to shelter. We finally ran out of places to go, and I ran out of hope. Then a miracle happened. Somebody sent me to Second Chance!

"It's hard to explain how I felt at that time. I had no hope, no confidence, no money, and no home. The people at Second Chance had an understanding of how women like me feel, and what we need. They did so much along the way to finding a good job for me. They found me an apartment, daycare for my children, work clothing, and they paid our expenses until my first paycheck arrived from my new job at the World Bank.

"In July of 2005, I released my first CD. After that I was interviewed by Voice of America, and I will be traveling around the world to promote my music.

"But besides all of this that can be seen and measured, Second Chance helped me to rebuild my hope and self-confidence, they gave me the moral support I needed to believe in my future and to never again be a victim of abuse."

Katherine

Katherine earned a Bachelor of Arts degree from Indiana University but stayed out of the workforce for over twenty years in order to care for her children. She was married to a man who lived a double life. During the day, he was a powerful attorney in Washington, D.C. At home, he had become a violent and verbally abusive husband and father, hurting his whole family.

The physical and emotional abuse increased in severity, until it became unbearable. "At some point," she said, "I realized my life was actually in danger." At about the same time, she found out about Second Chance through a friend who had also been abused and gone to Second Chance. "I knew she was out of her situation. Second Chance helped her get a job and she had a career. I saw she was supporting herself and her children."

Katherine was petrified of what would happen if she tried to leave her husband. She was afraid of what he would do to her, and what would happen to her children. "I assumed he was right that I could not support myself financially. I had a B.A. from Indiana University, but I hadn't worked for many years, to care for my children while my husband pursued his legal career." The abusive spouse had deprived her of her former self-confidence. She had been crushed by his routine attacks, and other abuse.

But her friend's success emboldened her to come to Second Chance.

"I started working at Starbuck's to pay for food and basic things, and Ludy Green advised me on long-term career goals. In the past, I'd worked as a free-lance photographer. Ludy could tell I loved photography. Thanks to her and the encouragement of others at Second Chance, I am now employed as a professional photographer with National Geographic, one of Second Chance's client partners.

"I'm doing the work I love and getting paid well. The income is more than sufficient to support my children without relying on my former husband. I can even pay legal bills for the divorce.

"Just a few months ago, when I lost hope of ever finding a better life, I did not think this was possible. Thank you Second Chance, and all the people who support this wonderful organization."

Maria

Maria was a hardworking, reliable mother of five with limited knowledge of English. She was seriously injured by her abusive spouse. She suffered from severe anxiety disorders as a result of years of abuse against her and her children.

Second Chance enrolled Maria in ESL classes to improve her communication skills. We connected her and her children with a psychologist service partner who provided years of tremendous counseling and support to bring emotional healing. We paid her first month's rent and security deposit for an apartment, and connected her with a service partner to give her family a computer and printer so her children could use them for homework; and another service partner repaired her computer and printer when it stopped working.

When we learned her children were sleeping on the floor, other service partners moved quickly to procure, deliver, and set up bunk beds and bedding for them. Another service partner donated a sewing machine to help Maria pursue her long-term dream of starting her own business as a seamstress.

We helped Maria obtain a job with a night-time office cleaning business, and later with a house cleaning company, where she became a team leader. After working successfully for almost a year, she called our office in tears. She found herself unable to resolve certain conflicts with fellow team members and superiors.

Our staff worked with both Maria and her superiors to ensure she learned and applied professional conflict resolution skills. Maria's aptitude for leadership and her flexibility in learning new skills allowed her to keep and excel in her job and her leadership position. She has since moved on to even better jobs, and her children have earned scholarships to competitive private schools in Washington, DC. The cycle of abuse stopped with Maria. She and her children are living in freedom from abuse in our nation's capital.

Lisa

Lisa is in her 40's and is a mother of three and also has a grandchild living with her. She was referred to Second Chance by Access Housing Chesapeake Veterans House. She had previously resided at Chesapeake House, but when she left there, she lived with an extremely violent boyfriend.

The Client Partner referred Lisa to Second Chance when he learned of our work because he knew of the violence she had suffered and that she needed extra help and advice in order to break free.

Her history with this violent boyfriend went back for several years. When she tried to leave, he stalked her, and spread lies about her at work which jeopardized her job. She ran out of money and ended up in domestic violence shelters and veterans' homeless shelters, separated from her children. She ended up back in the relationship, even after leaving the shelter.

When we met Lisa, she had just escaped from this abuser who at times held her at gunpoint in front of her children. When the abuser held a gun to her head, it was only the intervention of her 19-year-old son that saved her.

She came to us, desperately trying to hold her family together, keep a roof over their heads (without the abuser knowing where they were), go to school, and work to put food on the table.

We first encouraged her and provided her with the resources to seek a protective order. Second Chance then provided her with multiple trainings, numerous job referrals, interview coaching sessions, several job interviews with our partners, professional clothing, legal counseling, domestic violence counseling & service referrals, a pre-loaded cell phone, and so forth.

She obtained a job as a receptionist at Sanford Brown College, with a schedule that allows her to continue her education. We're continuing to forward her resume to partners such as: The State Department, VOX, and the Senate Committee on Environment and Public Works.

At one point, shortly after she started work at Sanford Brown, she called Second Chance saying that she hadn't been to work for 2 days because she didn't have any money for transportation. She couldn't get to our office to pick up funds. Second Chance tried wiring funds through western union, but the locations within walking distance to her had stopped providing services. Ultimately, the only option we saw for her to keep her job was for someone from Second Chance to drive to her home in Maryland (about an hour from the office), and drive her to work (another 45 minutes away). We also gave her the western union funds and she then had enough to carry her through till she received her paycheck.

She did not lose her job, and she has been working ever since! Second Chance expects to sponsor her for the WISP scholarship (it is available only to domestic violence survivors who have been working with a sponsoring domestic violence organization for at least six months), to help her with education costs and living expenses while she finishes school. Thanks to the wide range of individualized services Second Chance provided to Lisa, she is working and living independently today.

Kim

Kim, another client-survivor described her experience as follows:

> "I was referred to Second Chance by the Shelter that I was living in. They were there for me in a way no one else was. They didn't judge me. Through a job partner at George Washington University Hospital, they opened a door for me to a job opportunity that I wouldn't have had access to otherwise. They helped me every step of the way: providing me with childcare, transportation, a uniform for my job, and especially their continuous support.
>
> "If not for Second Chance, I would still be on welfare, taking classes daily for a stipend. Instead, I'm back in the workforce as a registered medical technician for George Washington University Hospital. I am able to provide for my children with a job I like that strengthens my skills and helps me to be a role model for them."

Pamela

Pamela, originally from Uganda, came to the United States as a small girl. The promises of freedom with which she had arrived were stolen by the man she married. He abused her and her three young sons. They lived in constant fear under his secret tyranny.

Pamela remained at home to raise her children, though she managed to earn a Bachelor's degree and to complete two years working towards a Master's degree in Accounting. Second Chance provided her with professional clothing, interview preparation and paid her transportation costs to and from job interviews. We helped her prepare a resume and send it to prospective employers.

The Association of American Medical Colleges (AAMC), one of our job partners, offered Pamela a position in their accounting department with a starting salary of $40,000 per year. After only six months at AAMC, she was already advancing within the company.

The President of AAMC had this to say with reference to Pamela's performance: "we have had the privilege of recently hiring one of these [Second Chance] candidates, who has become a valued member of our accounting staff." Today, Pamela is a successful working-mother of three, living with personal and financial security. She has never returned to the abusive partner.

Susan

Following is a paraphrase of the statement of Susan.

It had been nearly a year since I had obtained a restraining order against my husband and had him removed from the house. Though it took all of my emotional resources to accomplish this, I knew it was for the best.

With three kids, ages two, one, and just a few months, I was faced with financial, personal and professional crises. I lived for several months not knowing what would happen next. I had exhausted nearly all of my resources when I came to Second Chance. But before long I felt my life heading for an upswing.

Though Second Chance arranged many interviews for me, I was hard to place. My confidence had suffered. No job was forthcoming. But Second Chance didn't give up on me. Instead, they hired me on a part-time consulting basis to assist on training programs at Second Chance, which allowed me to demonstrate my skills to myself and others. Because Second Chance did not give up on me, even when I was giving up on myself, they were eventually able to help me get hired for a great managerial job with a national association. Now I see the concept of employment in a new light; and it is empowering! Second Chance helped me to turn my life around, and for this I will always be thankful.

Emma

A lack of work experience during the nearly 30 years she spent with her abusive spouse left Emma thinking it would be impossible for her to find a job. She describes her situation as follows.

"Resume after resume went out, seemingly into a black hole. I was desperate, and demoralized at not even getting one interview. . . . [M]ost employment agencies aren't interested in helping stay-at-home moms return to the workforce. They are not interested in the wealth of skills we have to offer. The only agency that took me seriously was Second Chance. Today, I have a great position at George Washington University. I'm looking toward to my future with a joy I haven't felt since childhood.

"Not only did [Second Chance] help me get a job, they also paid my commuting costs, and gave me two beautiful suits for my new position. As a result of these efforts and more, I'm finally regaining my self-confidence. I've never heard of another organization that helps women and their children the way Second Chance does. . . . In a sometimes dark world, Second Chance is a bright light."

Eugenia

She came to the United States for her son to receive treatment for a rare type of cancer in the eyes. After treatments in a Texas hospital, where Eugenia taught herself to speak English, her son eventually became blind. In addition to dealing with the trauma of a new country and her son's illness, Eugenia also faced severe abuse at the hands of her husband.

After separating from her husband, he began to threaten to take away her two sons. He continued these threats and harassment while Eugenia struggled desperately to find employment to secure the safety and security of her two sons. Eventually, Eugenia was referred to Second Chance by St. Matthew's Cathedral in Washington, DC. She arrived at our doors in a state of despair and hopelessness. There were times when Eugenia would begin to cry and felt as if she could not stop. She feared she had no choice but to go back to her abusive spouse, to avoid living in poverty and losing her sons. She was still under the influence of the vortex of abuse.

Second Chance and our partners helped her find housing, warm clothing, and legal assistance. We gave her vouchers for clothing for her children. She met with our staff frequently to draft resumes and practice her English and interviewing skills.

Eugenia began to feel less despair. With our help and support, she found a well-paying position caring for four children in a nice home. She now speaks English very well and is earning enough money to care for her children and send funds back to her aging parents in Peru, where she is from.

Joy

After their daughter was born, Joy and her former husband decided it would be best for her to quit her job and stay home to care for the children. "Gradually," Joy says "my husband became verbally and mentally abusive. He became controlling and possessive, going so far as nailing the windows of our house shut. Eventually, I had no freedom at all."

Unable to stand living this way, Joy bravely decided to leave. On a rainy night with $100 in her pocket, she packed up the kids and drove to a hotel where they lived for a few days before turning to relatives. Her former husband then began stalking her and taking their daughter for days at a time without Joy knowing their whereabouts. Being the strong woman that she is, Joy decided to take action. She pressed charges and got a restraining order against her husband.

Then Joy sought help from Child Protective Services, where she learned about WEAVE (Women Empowered Against Violence). It happened that WEAVE (now defunct) was a partner of Second Chance. They told Joy about us and referred her to us.

She thinks back on when she first came to Second Chance, "I was so surprised at how nice and supportive everyone was. They helped me update my résumé, they helped polish my rusty interviewing skills; they even got me a new suit and took me to get my hair done. They always made me feel I could succeed, and all of this helped me to regain my confidence."

"Then the real help came when Second Chance got me a job as a Financial Representative for SunTrust Bank. . . . I wouldn't have a job if it wasn't for Second Chance. They helped me to get my life started again." Joy has also been interviewed by CNN. She told them, "I hope that sharing my story will inspire others in my situation to get out and get help, and that it will encourage people to lend their support to Second Chance and the important work they do for women like me."

Teri

Teri left her husband who for many years had physically and verbally abused her and her children. She fled with her children to the safety of a friend's home in the Washington Metropolitan area.

Though she had many technological and administrative skills, Teri had been unemployed for many years. She was not current on the latest developments in her areas of experience. She tried to find jobs on her own without success. When she was referred to Second Chance by a client partner, she had no professional clothing suitable for interviews, and lacked housing and basic provisions necessary to survive. Through our service partners, Second Chance arranged for housing and the other items, including vouchers to obtain clothing for her children, and clothing for her to wear to interviews. Within a couple of weeks, she was employed by one of our job partners, who was in need of a person with administrative skills and a technological background.

Within a short time, Teri was promoted. The job partner called to thank us for recommending her, noting that her contribution was a "perfect fit." Teri told us that the employer treats her and her kids "like part of the family." Teri later updated her skills and moved on to a better paying position. She recently said, "I'll never forget the start that Second Chance gave me at the time I needed it most."

CHAPTER 17

The New VAWA and the Second Chance Provision

The unique success of Second Chance clients is not only a cause for hope but also a call to action. With over eight hundred of our clients having permanently terminated abusive relationships, breaking the cycle of violence, there can be no doubt that our approach works systematically and in a great variety of circumstances. At the same time, millions remain trapped under physical suffering and psychological trauma hardly to be imagined, and many children are traumatized daily as captive audiences to abuse. Having personal knowledge of an effective method for permanently liberating victims of domestic violence and human trafficking, how could I stand by and do nothing to expand the reach of our approach?

I have hopes of expanding the reach and resources of Second Chance, and also promoting the use of our approach by other agencies and organizations. If the Second Chance method is widely adopted, if there is an explosion of organizations replicating our techniques, I'm convinced we would enter a new era in the battle against these crimes. My aim is to make universal and ubiquitous the application of empowerment principles to domestic violence and trafficking victims. In so doing, I believe we can convert what is today still an epidemic into something rare or non-existent. With the track-record of our clients, I believe this goal is a real possibility that can be achieved. It is within our grasp.

A number of years ago, I became an active proponent of making public funds available to private non-profit businesses providing services like those of Second Chance. As I finish writing this book, my persistent efforts over the years are bearing fruit. Thanks to a successful lobbying effort on Capitol Hill, my vision of federal funding for the Second Chance approach is now a provision in the Violence Against Women Act.

The Violence Against Woman Act provides federal authority for important programs and initiatives against domestic violence. It authorizes, for example, investigations and prosecutions of violent crimes against women; allows for civil remedies in cases that are not criminally prosecuted; establishes a national hotline for victims; and promotes local programs in communities throughout the nation. The VAWA provides funding for legal service agencies, such as the Legal Aid Society of the District of Columbia, to help protect victims by obtaining court-ordered protective orders against abusers.

Originally passed in 1994, the VAWA was reauthorized three times, most recently in March of 2013. During the period leading up to this latest renewal, with the pro bono assistance of attorneys Jon S. Bouker and James A. Hunter, partner and director, respectively, at the law firm of Arent Fox, I met with members of the House of Representatives and the Senate Judiciary Committee. After explaining the work of Second Chance and our results, I advocated specific language for inclusion in the VAWA that would allow nonprofit businesses to apply for federal grants to fund employment training and placement services for domestic violence victims.

As a direct result of this effort, the 2013 reauthorization includes a provision that, for the first time, makes federal funds available to organizations providing employment services to victims of domestic violence. Chapter 11, Subtitle B now authorizes grants for qualifying organizations to provide "employment counseling, occupational training, job retention counseling, and counseling on re-entry into the workforce."

Because the purpose is to enhance resources available to Second Chance and also to facilitate the use of my approach by other organizations, I refer to it as the Second Chance Provision. The new provision expressly includes funding for organizations that provide "job retention counseling, and counseling on re-entry into the workforce." The emphasis on lasting employment—careers with purpose and meaning, consistent with the employee's interests and talents, and with the pursuit of her dreams, all in the difficult context of surviving domestic abuse—this is an essential Second Chance innovation. Job retention is a key component in the system that empowers survivors for lasting freedom, preventing them from ever going back to abuse.

Regardless of one's political views, funds available through the Second Chance Provision is, I believe, an appropriate use of tax money, given the enormous societal burdens of domestic violence and human trafficking. Domestic violence costs the U.S. economy a staggering $5 to $8 billion annually. The expenditures allocated for these grants are infinitesimal by comparison, yet have the potential to greatly reduce the economic and human costs of these crimes. They will serve as an investment to continue the spread of a program that has proven effective in empowering survivors to become financially independent.

I've been heartened to see a growing number of organizations adopting the Second Chance model, offering employment training and placement services, with rising awareness of underlying principles, and emphasis on the importance of personal calling and meaningful employment. By following the methods outlined in this book, and securing grants under the new VAWA provision, the physical, economic and emotional stranglehold of abusers can be systematically disrupted, and stopped on a national scale. The Second Chance Provision, can help provide the necessary resources needed in the effort to end domestic violence and human trafficking.

Endnotes

1. Isaiah 40:31.
2. Adams, Adrienne E., Cris M. Sullivan, Deborah Bybee, Megan R. Greeson. "Development of the Scale of Economic Abuse." *Violence Against Women*. Vol. 14, no. 5 (May 2008): 563-588.
3. Adams et al. (2008) at 569.
4. Additional information may be found in an article about my role in the new provision published shortly after the bill was signed into law. Hopkins, Christopher Snow. "The Violence Against Women Act Started With One Woman: Ludy Green." *National Journal*, May 30, 2013. http://www.nationaljournal.com/daily/the-violence-against-women-act-started-with-one-woman-ludy-green-20130311.
5. CDC Report, *Op cit.*
6. Letter dated December 14, 2011 from Linda C. Degutis, Director, CDC's National Center for Injury Prevention and Control.
7. CDC Report at 1. http://www.cdc.gov/ViolencePrevention/intimatepartnerviolence/index.htm
8. "Survey: 1 in 4 Women Victims of Severe Violence." Associated Press, December 14, 2011, http://www.cbsnews.com/news/survey-1-in-4-women-victims-of-severe-violence/
9. Blog post at "Elders Blog" of former President Jimmy Carter, November 25, 2013. *Marking the International Day for the Elimination of Violence Against Women*, http://theelders.org/article/women-live-profoundly-different-more-dangerous-world

10. Rice, Max W, E. Finkelstein, R.A. Bardwell, and S. Leadbetter. "The Economic Toll of Intimate Partner Violence Against Women in the United States." *Violence and Victims.* Vol. 19, no. 3 (2004): 259–72. The cost includes medical care, mental health services, and lost productivity. *Costs of Intimate Partner Violence Against Women in The United States* (CDC Atlanta: March 2003). www.cdc.gov.violenceprevention/pdf/IPVBook-a-pdf.

11. "The National Intimate Partner and Sexual Violence Survey: Summary Report, Executive Summary)" (Atlanta: Center for Disease Control 2010): 1. http://www.cdc.gov/violenceprevention/pdf/nisvs_executive_summary-a.pdf

12. Walker, Lenore E. *The Battered Woman Syndrome.* (New York: Springer Publishing Co. 1984) , 119. See also Pizzey, Erin, *Scream Quietly or the Neighbors Will Hear.* (London: Penguin 1974).

13. Eccl 4:3.

14. Eccl. 4:1.

15. McDonald, P. Lynn. "Helping to End the Assaultive Relationship" *in* B. Pressman, Cameron, G. and Rothery, M. (eds.), *Intervening with Assaulted Women: Current Theory, Research and Practice.* (Waterloo: Laurier University 1989),111–124.

16. Barnett, Ola W. and Alyce D. LaViolette. *It Could Happen to Anyone: Why Battered Women Stay.* (Newberry, CA: 1st Ed., Sage Publications 1993), :76.

17. McDonald (1989), *supra,* at 93.

18. "The Sean Hannity Show" (Broadcast September 21, 2011) http://www.hannity.com/show/2011/09/21

19. Bard, Marjorie. *Organizational and Community Responses To Domestic Abuse and Homelessness* (New York: Garland Publishing 1994), 56.

20. Ms. Sheehan was convicted on a lesser weapons charge.

21. Walker, Lenore. *The Battered Woman* (New York: Harper Colophon 1980), 83 *et seq.*

22. Subsequent studies suggest that while the cycle of violence theory describes commonly occurring aspects of these relationships, it is in some respects incomplete.

23. Walker (1980), supra, at 189.

24. The term "domestic tyranny" gained some popularity in the 1980s as a result of Elizabeth Hafkin Pleck's important work of that name. *Domestic Tyranny: The Making of American Social Policy Against Family Violence from Colonial to the Present,* (Oxford University Press 1984, *reprinted,* University of Illinois Press 2004).

25. "Eric Schmidt's daughter lifts lid on 'very strange' North Korea," *The Telegraph* January 22, 2013. http://www.telegraph.co.uk/technology/google/9817335/Eric-Schmidts-daughter-lifts-lid-on-very-strange-North-Korea.html

26. *Id.*

27. http://www.cdc.gov/ViolencePrevention/intimatepartnerviolence/index.html

28. Adams *et al.* (2008) *at* 568.

29. *Id. at* 565

30. *Id.* at 564

31. *Id.* at 565 and studies cited.

32. *Id.* at 565 and studies cited.

33. *Id.* at 566

34. *Id.* at 565

35. *Id.* at 567

36. *Id.* at 567

37. *Id.*

38. *Id.*

39. The State Department's website, http://www.state.gov/j/tip/ ("Trafficking in Persons Report"), contains information about the nature of the crimes and efforts in the United States and around the world to prosecute offenders and protect victims.

40. *United Nations Protocol to Prevent, Suppress and Punish Trafficking in Persons, Especially Women and Children, supplementing the United Nations Convention against Transnational Organized Crime* Article 3 (a).

41. U.S. Department of State, *Trafficking in Persons Report,* http://www.state.gov/j/tip/rls/tiprpt/countries/2013/215511.htm (2013)

42. *Id.*

43. Aiken, Jane H. and Katherine Goldwasser, "The Perils of Empowerment," 20 *Cornell J.L. & Pub. Pol'y* 139 (2010), 169–170.
44. *Id.*
45. http://www.raptoreducationgroup.org/View_Newsupdate.cfm?title_bar=Student's%20Track%20Rehabilitated%20Bald%20Eagles%20-%20March%202001&NewsID=17
46. Letter from Thomas Jefferson to Mrs. Anna Scott Marks, July 12, 1788, reprinted in Sarah N. Randolph, *The Domestic Life of Thomas Jefferson*, DSI Digital Reproduction (Scituate, MA 2001), 135.
47. Fyodor Dostoevsky, *The House of the Dead*.
48. Client partners are listed on Second Chances website at http://www.scesnet.org/partners/client_partners.php
49. Job partners are listed on Second Chances website at http://www.scesnet.org/partners/job_partners.php)

Ludy Green, Ph.D.

Dr. Ludy Green is one of the world's foremost experts on violence against women and children. She speaks regularly in national and international venues on the importance of financial autonomy in breaking the abusive patterns that hold captive victims of violence and human trafficking, and she is a contributing writer on women's issues for the *Huffington Post*.

The methodology pioneered by Dr. Green has been validated by the work of the non-profit organization she founded in 2001, Second Chance Employment Services. Second Chance's innovative program has been uniquely successful in helping hundreds of survivors attain lifelong freedom from domestic violence and human trafficking through financial and emotional independence.

Second Chance is the nation's first and only employment placement agency for domestic violence and human trafficking victims. In its thirteen years of operation, Second Chance has expanded from its home base in Washington, DC to operations in New York, Atlanta, Los Angeles, and other locations, and has become one of the leading domestic violence prevention programs in the United States. The service model of Second Chance has been adopted by federal agencies and is the basis for public education campaigns, policy development, and leadership training for preventing and ending violence against women and children, around the nation and worldwide.

Under Dr. Green's direction, Second Chance Employment Services was a driving force behind passage in March 2013 of a key provision within the reauthorized Violence Against Women Act. The Act, first passed in 1994, and reauthorized in 2000, 2005, and 2013, was the nation's first comprehensive federal response to the violence that plagues families and communities. Last year's renewal included a landmark provision advocated by Dr. Green to allocate federal funds for organizations that provide employment services for victims of domestic violence and human trafficking. Dr. Green is now leading an effort to pass the International Violence Against Women Act to prevent gender-based violence on a global scale.

Dr. Green was appointed by the U.S. Department of State to serve as Cultural Ambassador of the United States in Human Trafficking to Jordan and Syria in 2009. She served as a U.S. Delegate to Malaysia (2013), Turkey (2011), Chile (2009), and at the Global Summit of Women Vietnam (2008). November 2013, she was a presenter at the Qatar International Business Women Forum in Qatar. In 2006 she was appointed by the U.S. Attorney General to the Advisory Council of Domestic Violence Against Women. Dr. Green was also appointed to the Board of Trustees for the Family and Children's Trust Fund of Virginia; elected to serve on the Commission of the Status of Women in Virginia; and elected to the Economic Development Commission in the District of Columbia.

For her work in domestic violence and human trafficking Dr. Green's numerous awards include: Nominee to the United Nations Business Leader's Award, Fight Human Trafficking in Luxor, Egypt (2011); *Washington Business Journal's* Women Who Mean Business Award (2010); Brava Award (2009); Woman of Vision Award (2008); Washingtonian of the Year (2008); U.S. Attorney General's Professional Innovation in Victims Services (2007); "Volvo for Life Award" (2006); Human Resource Association of the National Capital Area's "HR

Leader Award for Excellence in Community Service" (2005); Toyota and ABC Channel 7's "Tribute to Working Women Award (2005).

Fluent in French, Spanish, Portuguese, Italian and German, Dr. Green has a B.S. in International Finance; she earned her M.A. in Human Resources Management and Ph.D. in Industrial Organization Psychology from George Washington University. She graduated from the Leadership Washington Program in 2003, and Finance for Senior Executives at Harvard University in 2010. She is a long-standing member of the Society of Human Resources Management; the International Women Forum ("IWF"); and the Women's Forum of New York and Washington, DC.

Dr. Green resides in Washington, DC with her husband Joseph S. Green and their daughter Megan.

Other Books on Domestic Violence by Volcano Press

Learning to Live Without Violence: *A Handbook for Men*
Dr. Daniel Sonkin and Dr. Michael Durphy

Aprender a Vivir Sin Violencia: *Manual Para Hombres*
(Learning to Live Without Violence, Spanish Edition)

Surviving Domestic Violence: *Voices of Women Who Broke Free*
Elaine Weiss

Family and Friends' Guide to Domestic Violence: *How to Listen, Talk and Take Action When Someone You Care About is Being Abused*
Elaine Weiss

Physician's Guide to Intimate Partner Violence and Abuse: *A Reference for All Health Care Professionals*
Ellen Taliaferro, M.D. and Patricia Salber, M.D.

Testifying Under Oath: *How to be an Effective Witness*
James Vukelic

Child Abuse and Neglect: *Guidelines for Identification, Assessment, and Case Management*
(Edited by) Marilyn Peterson and Michael Durfee

For ordering:
www.volcanopress.com
sales@volcanopress.com

volcanopress.com

Volcano Press
Box 270
Volcano, CA 95689